THE BUILDING OF MIRACLES

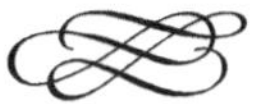

J. L. RAYMOND

This book is dedicated to The Barbs, David and Whit, Al and Don D., and all of the other members and volunteers that sacrificed financially and physically to build this church so that they could have a place to freely gather, commune, pray, and express themselves, and praise God the way they want to in safety and not feel in danger of being ridiculed themselves and for future generations.

EPIGRAPH

Coming together is a beginning, staying together is progress,
and working together is success.

–

Henry Ford

ACKNOWLEDGMENTS

~

I am sure everyone has heard the saying, "It takes a village to raise a child." Well, it takes a melting pot to build a church of God's Gay people. It also takes a village to write a book about building a church.

I had been wanting to write this book for decades, but I didn't really even know where to start and what to do from there.

I am grateful to Emily Shurr at Mental Temple for getting me started.

I want to thank David Williams, who was a major contributor to the construction of the building, as were so many other people. He is also one of the few still alive and was able to help me verify incidences of events that I wanted to make sure were correct. He also read a copy of the manuscript as it was being shaped into a book and his comments were extremely helpful.

There are also two other people that mean alot to me, Buzzy and Lynn Wiseman, at Cactus Jack's RV Park in Salt Springs, Florida. They helped with the reading of the manuscript and helped me correct my grammar in the beginning!

I want to thank my wife, Lona, for her support during the times of recalling friends who were no longer alive.

I also want to acknowledge and make a huge thank you to Angel Woods, ghostwriter/editor, and her husband. He was very supportive by giving his wife and me the best computer to do the job.

I truly want to honor everyone involved with the building of the church and helping to create this book!

PREFACE

This book is about how a special group of 12 people, meeting in the personal home of a Lesbian couple, laid the groundwork for something so spectacular that it needs to be told. The hurdles that had to be overcome within the church and by the public outside of the church simply ***must*** be brought to the light. Though some of the names in this book are fictitious, all the people are real and actually made the following events happen over a period of almost 10 years.

I was called by God in 1990 to help this group of people finish the construction of the building they had started, but didn't know how to complete. ***This is a true story.*** Even though the building was completed more than 30 years ago, it is still the most amazing and cherished experience of my life.

I have wanted to share this story for a long time, but I always found an excuse to not do it. However, over the years we have lost many of the people involved with the creation, planning, contributing, and erecting of this building. Since we are all much older now and some have died, or are of poor and declining health, I want to make the world aware of this event and to memorialize the participants of this fantastic blessing. I hope you enjoy.

CONTENTS

INTRODUCTION

~

In 1968, a cleric named Troy Perry, Jr. was in a bar in Los Angeles visiting a friend of his. There was a raid, and several people were arrested for being Gay. They didn't arrest Troy, but it was at ***that*** moment he ***knew*** God loved him and God loved Gay people, as well. God didn't discriminate. He created all of His children equally, and He loved them all.

That same night, Troy saw a Gay publication titled "The Advocate." He asked the bartender how to get in touch with the editor of this paper. He wanted to run an ad.

Troy wanted to start a church!

The bartender told him the editors would be arriving to write an article about the raid. Troy was there when they came in. He told the paper representative he wanted to take out an ad for a church he wanted to start. At first, the paper denied him. They had so many straight organizations attempting to place ads in it to condemn Gay people that they wouldn't let him do it.

After about 30 minutes of his preaching to the editor about how he wanted to bring it forward to Gay people, that God loved them all, and that he was going to start the church out of his house, "The Advocate" agreed. The following Sunday, Troy held the first service from his home.

On the first night, 12 people showed up. There wasn't a dry eye at the end of the service. The next week it was down to 10, and then eight. However, by the end of 1971, there were more than 1,000 in attendance.

This whole story of Troy Perry's was related in an interview with Troy himself on YouTube. He told all about the raid, the start of the church, and its growth to what it is today. There are several others that can be watched to learn about Troy Perry, Jr.

https://www.youtube.com/watch?v=gNajAvP0nhA

The church that Troy Perry Jr. founded is called Metropolitan Community Church and has a ministry of Lesbian, Gay, Bi-sexual, and Transgender communities. It started in L.A. in 1968 and gradually went global. Perry retired as MCC's Moderator in 2005 and was succeeded by Nancy Wilson as the second Moderator – and the first female Moderator. Today, nearly 60 years after its founding, there are 222 affiliated churches in 37 countries connected to MCC.

In the early '80s, an organization called "Gay Talk" held meetings at Quaker Meeting House in Gainesville, Florida. Among the group were several of the founding members of Trinity Metropolitan Church, who will be mentioned often throughout this book. This story is basically our legacy to be remembered. It tells how all of this project came about and was finished by the volunteering labor of the church members over a period of almost 10 years.

On occasion, some of the people at Gay Talk would go to St. Luke's MCC in Jacksonville, Florida to attend their worship services with Rev. Don D. Jackson (also referred to as D.J.). D.J. came to Gainesville once, and after that the deacons would come down to speak to the "Gay Talk" group and saw several familiar faces in the audience. Many of these people became friends, and the group continued to grow.

Whit Gibson was originally from Tampa, Florida. He had fond memories of his former connection to the Tampa MCC, where he sang in the choir. It was an open, loving community where LGBTQ people of many faith backgrounds, or no faith background at all, could be themselves and grow in so many ways.

Gay Talk was the only comparable community in Gainesville. Over time, as D.J. got to know Whit, he felt that Gainesville would benefit from an MCC. He presented the idea of an LGBTQ church in Gainesville that would be welcoming to all.

In 1983, Whit and his partner, David Williams, went to the Florida MCC District Conference and spoke with Reverend Arthur Fleschner, the district coordinator. He urged the group to work with the Jacksonville church to get one started in Gainesville. Much like Troy Perry had started MCC in LA in his house in 1968 with 12 attendees, the Gainesville MCC church started on August 14, 1983, in a Lesbian couple's home with 12 attendees. It was officiated by Reverend Jackson. For a while, a few of the Jacksonville deacons would come to Gainesville to hold services. By 1984, the group was able to hire a pastor.

It was commonly referred to during the construction of this building about the similarity of the twelves. 12 apostles, 12 founding members of Troy's church, and 12 founding members of the Gainsville church. It was almost like it was a sign.

After two meetings in a private home, they were able to rent one of the Sunday School classrooms at the Unitarian Church. By 1984, the MCC group had outgrown the classroom, so they rented the main sanctuary of the church in the evenings. They stayed there until 1991. In 1986, the MCC issued the Gainesville church a charter. They were now officially called Trinity Metropolitan Community Church (TMCC), an affiliate church of Troy Perry's Universal Fellowship MCC, which he had started in LA back in 1968.

In 1985, TMCC church started talking about buying a church, but they couldn't afford a building. They held many fundraisers, but after trying to buy the building they wanted, and being unable to work a deal, they decided to build their own church.

In 1986, they signed a purchase agreement for five acres of land in the name of the church. It was a blessing for them to get this property, as they found an owner who was willing to hold financing for this new church entity with so little money.

In 1987, one of the church members was a contractor and obtained their permit from the City of Gainesville Building Department. They made it very difficult to get the permit because of the type of building it was, a quonset hut—or more likely, because it was going to be a Gay church. The contractor was an elderly man and made it clear he wasn't able to do anything on the project. The volunteers understood and were fine with that.

Later that year, the congregation members pooled their skills (of which there were few) and organized work parties to prepare the property for construction. They now had the land but no money to build, so, ultimately, the congregation stepped up and cleared the land themselves for the building and parking area. Others who couldn't do that kind of work created fundraisers for the cause.

Other members dug the foundation or pulled up the arches for the quonset building. That building style was chosen for its sturdier structure to withstand hurricanes and its very low maintenance. They hung drywall, painted, and everything else that didn't require a licensed subcontractor. The building construction progressed as long as the money lasted. Then, the building construction would come to a halt until more money could be raised.

Two members of the church purchased a single-wide mobile home and moved it onto the property to serve as a combined church office and pastor's office. The permanent water and septic system for the mobile home and the main church were installed at that time. Temporary power poles for both buildings were installed at that time, as well.

In 1990, the volunteers hit the wall that many had anticipated. The contractor who pulled the permit had told them up front that he would pull the permit, but couldn't do anything to help with the building because he didn't really know how to bend the drywall on the steel walls for the building or to how to complete the interior of the building.

When the question was taken to the engineer at the start of construction, they didn't know what to do to make it happen, either.

The company they bought the building from didn't have any idea of how to insulate and bend drywall on such a curved wall. They reminded the church volunteers that these buildings were primarily used for farming equipment or other industrial purposes and were not typically finished for any type of attractive aesthetic use.

In 1983, people were brave enough to come to the initial meetings required to create a church of their own. They went through many hoops to become one. There were donors who wanted to be able to contribute to the church and Building Fund but were fearful of writing checks out to Trinity MCC, for fear their check would be recognized as being written to a Gay organization.

While this was a setback, some of the volunteers had basic framing skills. They framed the end walls and bathrooms and continued working on things they could do until the next miracle happened. As if this congregation had not already been blessed with so many miracles to get to this point, they were not giving up this late in the game!

This is where I came in and where the real magic brings all these miracles together for this church and its members. It's already an amazing miracle that these people had made it so far on their own. I will be sharing how it came to this point and the miracles and love that brought it all together.

I truly believe that all the things that happened to me in my youth, my education, my work ethic, and my surrendering to God's call, even though I had no idea of who He was, all prepared me for this specific mission with these wonderful people, this community, and the other people that have been touched through the creation of this church over the years.

CHAPTER ONE
MIRACLE #1: GETTING THE CALL FROM GOD, 1990

It all started for me in the Spring of 1990. I lived in the southeast area of downtown Gainesville during this time, and I very seldom found the need to go to the other end of town. This one evening, I found myself driving north on what is known as Millhopper Road, or NW 43rd Street. It is a busy part of town, and I have never cared for busy sections. For some reason, though, there I was. Little did I know that there was going to be a miracle about to happen to me—one that would affect me and hundreds of others for the rest of our lives!

I believe I was in the left lane of the four-lane section of the road, but I'm not sure why. I was waiting in line to get through a red light. When the light changed, my truck immediately made a left turn into a parking lot across the street. I don't even know whether traffic was clear or why and how my truck was turning. ***I had no control of the steering of my truck!*** What makes it even weirder was that my truck was a five-speed on the floor, but I wasn't giving it gas, doing the clutch, or changing gears. I had no idea where I was turning into, but I didn't really have a choice. ***The truck was going into this parking lot!*** As I got into the parking lot, I realized it was pretty crowded... and I had no idea why I was there.

I didn't have to drive around the parking lot at all. There was one open parking spot, right in front of this building. ***The truck went straight to it!*** I had to take a few minutes to catch my breath and try to figure out what had just happened. Of course, I ***had*** to be by myself! Who would believe what just happened to me?

As I sat there, I realized I was at the front door of a church, but it was very dark inside. I thought it was closed, which confused me even more. The sign over the door said "Unitarian Community Church," and I thought, "What the hell am I doing here?" As I was trying to give my brain an answer to that question, I noticed some very dim lights inside, so I figured I would go in to see what this place was and maybe get an answer to my question.

When I went in, it was a very quaint church, and very dark. There were a few dimmed sconce lights on the side walls, and there was a female preacher giving a sermon. I had never seen or heard of a female preacher! As I looked around, I could see that every seat in the room was occupied, and that it appeared to be mostly Gay people in the room. I thought, "This must be the Gay church I have been hearing about, but why am I here?"

I also noticed that all the side walls were covered by people standing up to listen to the service. I figured I would possibly find a spot against the wall, as well. As I turned to my right to start working my way into a potential spot, a couple of ladies started waving me over showing me there was an empty seat right in front of them and they wanted me to take it. I went over and sat in the seat.

Not even five minutes into listening to this preacher, I started bawling my eyes out—and I hated crying! I couldn't stop the tears, no matter how hard I tried. All I could do was pray that the lights didn't come back up before they stopped. To this day, I don't have a single idea as to anything this preacher talked about. It went on for about 15 minutes, and it seemed like an eternity! I'm sure it was good.

When the sermon was over and the lights started coming up, I dried my eyes and got myself composed before anyone saw me. My intention was to just stand up and turn around and leave, but that plan didn't happen. This group was very friendly with each other. They hugged each other and said goodbye to everyone. Apparently, a few noticed I was new to the church, so they wanted to welcome me—which delayed my escape plan.

As it worked out, my seat—the only seat that had been available—was right next to a member named Barb. Just as I was starting my escape plan, the woman I was seated next to reached out to shake my hand. "My name is Barb Haws. My partner's name is Barb Canning. Everyone refers to us as 'the Barbs.' They call my partner Big Barb because she's about 5'9". They call me Little Barb because I'm about 5'4". What's your name?"

I told her my name was Judy. She asked me what I did for a living, and I told her I was a contractor who graduated from UF (University of Florida). She said, "Really?" I said "Yes." She then told me, "You may just be the answer to my prayers," and I responded with a quick chuckle. I said, "I seriously doubt that," and laughed once again.

She said "No, seriously." She then told me that this group was actually part of another church called Trinity Metropolitan Community Church. "We're renting this church until we can get our church built. We're building our own church by using volunteers from our congregation, but we're stuck on where to go from where we are."

She continued: "I'm the head of the building committee for the church, and we're building a steel quonset building. We have the slab and all the arches are up, but the contractor that pulled the permit for us doesn't know how to complete the interior the way we want to. We want to maintain the curve of the building. The architect and engineer don't know what to do, either. So I have been praying for God to bring us someone that can help us with that." She then asked me, "Can I take you out for a cup of coffee, show you the drawings, and talk to you about it? I'd like to see if you would come out to look at it?" I responded, "I don't drink coffee, but I will have a glass of tea with you and see what I can do to help, if anything."

We made an appointment to meet the following Tuesday to look at the drawings and discuss the many issues they had run into and then I went home.

CHAPTER TWO
WHY ME, GOD?

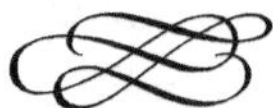

As I was driving home I was like "What just happened? My truck just took me to this church and now I'm supposed to build this quonset hut? I don't know God, I don't know Jesus!! Why me?

"What is going to make them trust me? ***Why*** are they going to trust me? They don't even know me. Hell, ***I*** don't even know me. Do Gay people even actually ***have*** churches? If there is a God up there, please tell me what's going on? Is this real or am I asleep? How did You take my truck away?

"I'm glad You introduced me to Barb first. I will definitely need her to be on my side. I have never done anything like this. The congregation took on all this construction work with no experience and here I am ***with*** construction experience and a degree and I'm the nervous one about stepping in because I don't know why I was chosen. Okay, God, I will step in and see what we can do, but ***please*** don't bail on me. It is obvious these people want this done. They have been working on it for years. Okay. Yeah. We will do it!!"

~

Even to this day during the writing of this book, I still don't know why I was chosen, but I did find God!

~

CHAPTER THREE
LEARNING THE HISTORY OF THE BUILDING AND WHERE THEY ARE HUNG UP

We met as scheduled, and she brought me up to speed about how they had acquired the land and purchased pre-engineered drawings for a quonset building. I was impressed with the site. It was a beautiful wooded 5-acre lot, and it had this really cool 32-by-60-foot quonset hut building sitting in the middle of it. These are typically used as low-maintenance farm storage buildings, but because Florida gets a lot of hurricanes, they wanted it to be very strong.

I got a lot of information from Little Barb that evening, basically the history of getting to where they were now. A member of the church was a building contractor that pulled the building permit, but he made it clear that he wasn't in a position to help them do any of the work. They understood and agreed. I told her up front, "I have never worked on a quonset building before, but I'm impressed with where you have gotten, and I would like to be a part of it."

Little Barb was showing me the property and told me that the first work day had happened in May 1987. All the members of the church had been so excited in the beginning and had gotten so much work done! They cut down the fence and cleared the entrance of bushes and small trees. They also removed about 50 larger trees for the building site and parking area, but they left it very nicely wooded. Even though the entrance was at one of the busiest roads in Gainesville, you could hardly hear the traffic, because they had kept a nice thick area of vegetation along the road.

As little Barb had already told me, this project had been constructed by the church members and volunteers. As I walked around with her and learned more of how they had gotten to this point, I was impressed with the progress they had made on their own. Most of the labor had been done by people who really had no experience in construction.

Talk about a leap of faith!

Here's what it looked like when I got there the first day and it felt like an oven when I walked in!

Shortly after the construction had gotten underway, the pastor had resigned for personal reasons. This had slowed the momentum of the building progress, but the people were not going to let it stop them. The ongoing clearing and working on the property continued while the search for a new pastor and the process for getting permits continued.

The congregation was adamant on building the church! So once final decisions were made by the congregation and the board of the Building Committee, the building funds grew and became sufficient to have the building materials for the arches delivered to the site in September of 1988.

With permits in hand and arches delivered, the congregation

volunteers were motivated to get back to work digging the footings and placing the rebar on the site. All of the footings were deeper than they needed to be, but again, the volunteers were very excited. The church had hired a company to prep the slab and place the concrete.

After the concrete had been poured and the arches were on the site, everyone got very excited all over again. They were so happy to have a slab and all the building parts. Little Barb, David and Whit, and another member, named Ernie, all got together, read the assembly instructions from the company, and worked out a plan on how to get the arches put together and raised into place.

In March 1989, Ernie and many other volunteers had raised the first arch using ropes. Marsha Millett was one of the volunteers on the site. In a history tracking document kept by the church, she was quoted as saying, "Pulling the first arch up was a trip and a half!"

Little Barb gave me a VHS tape (remember, this was the '80s) so I could see the raising and placement of the arches. —quite a scary part of the video! I think I would have used different words than ***"a trip and a half..."*** something more like "***terrifying***" comes to mind!

This is the first arch being pulled up. You can see it is warping! Just a little glimpse of the "terrifying" part!

The document described the raising of the first arch as follows:

"The heavy arch weighed 250 pounds and was 32 feet wide. Church members held each end and lifted the swaying arch until they were able to attach it to the slab. It was daunting, to say the least. Ernie and the volunteers used ropes to hoist the flexing, twisting, and otherwise totally uncooperative arch into place and secure it.

... It was just more proof that God wanted this building built and that He was truly watching over His people, because they pulled this part off without any injuries! ***This was probably one of the original miracles in making this building happen—before I even arrived on the scene.***

The Metropolitan Community Church district coordinator came up from South Florida to witness the event, and the new church reverend arrived three months later to witness the placing of the final arch.

Whit being his fearless self during the arches raising.

That Saturday, when little Barb and I arrived at the building site, there were four or five people working on framing in the front and rear ends of the structure for the entries. They were about 80% complete on getting them dried in, and they had the interior walls for the bathrooms and kitchen framed in, as well. Little Barb was taking me around to meet the people involved.

Sue and her partner. Both were very dedicated to the building of the church.

One woman was working on the front wall. Little Barb introduced me to her as Sue. Little Barb told her I was looking around to see what I could do to help. Little Barb told me that Sue and Whit had gotten the framing done up to that point. She had some construction experience and walked with us to show me what had been accomplished so far. She confirmed that constructing anything on the structure from this point was above her pay grade and that she had no idea how to proceed forward. She would be very happy if I could figure it out, and would help any way she could.

She also told me that she was a student at UF studying computer programming, that she would be graduating in a couple of months, and that she and her partner would be relocating. She had already accepted a job with a tech company in Arkansas. Talk about being in on the ground floor of the computer era! I thanked her for all the intel and said I looked forward to working with her. I was glad she would be around, at least for a little while, in case I had questions.

Whit

Two men were working on the rear wall. Little Barb introduced me to one of them, named Whit Gibson. She told him I was looking around and thought I might be able to help. He just looked at me and made the comment, "I'll believe it when I see it." I didn't quite know how to take it at that time, but then I thought, I'm sure they have heard those words a lot from many people and there had been no follow-through or maybe he just saw this young girl coming in and saying she knew something and assumed she was to never be seen again.

As I got to know Whit, I realized that was

just Whit. He had no fear or filters. You always knew where you stood with him. You either learned to love Whit or avoid him. I learned to love and respect him a lot. He had a lot of handy skills with construction, so he could be assigned to various projects with little oversight. He was also a very kind and generous soul, but never boasted about what he could do.

David, 1991

I also met David Williams that day. He was working on the rear wall with Whit. He was Whit's partner for over 20 years. They were two major supporters to the church, and they were at the site every Saturday. He was the polar opposite of Whit. He was more friendly and kinder with his words. They were just opposite enough to be a great couple.

Little Barb introduced me to him and told him I was looking around and thought I might be able to help. His response was, "Oh, that would be nice. We could sure use some help! We hope to see you again."

I thought to myself, "Talk about 'opposites attract!'"

I started meeting some of the other volunteers, learning their skills, and making plans for how we were going to progress through this project. It was quite an interesting undertaking working with unskilled or limited-skill workers, and I was really excited at figuring out how to make these walls bend—I knew I would figure it out.

I also met Al Miller and Don D. on my first official workday. I called Donald "Don D." from the beginning. I just liked the name. Al was Al. Al had been coming to the church for a while, and Don D. was relatively new to the church. He and Al had been partners for a year or two. They were

Al and Don D.

very much in love and completely dedicated to the church.

The whole property maintenance was taken care of by many of the members, but it didn't take long to see that Al, Whit, or Little Barb were the primary caretakers of the property, but I had a plan for Al down the road. For right now, just keeping it mowed was going to be all that mattered.

Little Barb and I walked through the building for a couple of hours, and I reminded her I had never worked on a quonset hut building. Given a little time, though, I thought I could figure it out and that we could get it finished in about a year or a little longer.

My main concerns were about the lack of money in the Building Fund and the need for more volunteers to do the work.

In response to these concerns, she told me that if there was hope of being able to actually get the building completed in the near future, there would be more contributors, and all the money and volunteers would be there. It kind of sounds like the movie *Field of Dreams*, doesn't it?

CHAPTER FOUR
IDENTIFYING PROBLEMS AND FIXING THEM

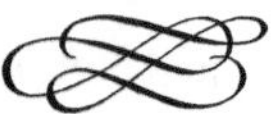

On my initial walk-through with Little Barb, I discovered and informed her, right off the bat, they could stop framing the front and rear end walls. There needed to be a major change to the concrete under the front and rear walls. Also, the bottom plate they installed was not pressure-treated and would have to be replaced before they could proceed. I explained to them what needed to happen to correct an error that was in the drawings for the slab and what to do to remove the bottom plate. They stopped what they were doing and started to prepare to make the changes for the corrections.

As I talked to Little Barb more about the floor plan, I asked why there was no plan for an office space for the preacher or an assistant or just storage. Since we had to do that concrete pour, we could get a concrete person to come in and form up the slab and footings for that. I put together an addendum drawing for a 12-by-24-foot room addition at the back of the church building for Little Barb to take to the engineer to sign off.

Little Barb had to first present the plan to the Building Committee, so she called a special meeting to get approval. She asked me to attend. The committee was there and liked the idea, but the pastor was adamant on denying it. She was concerned about how difficult it was to get funding on what we had going on already and thought an addition was a bad idea.

I presented to them that the addition would be such a small building that we would get a better price on the concrete needed for the end walls of the main sanctuary. Now would be the cheapest time to build the addition. If we waited, we would have to do demolition on the existing building to build the new addition. This way, it would be an easy framing job that could be wired at the same time as the main building instead of having to cut holes in walls later.

The committee voted for the room addition, so Little Barb moved forward with submitting the drawings to the engineer for approval and stamping. When that was done, she submitted it to the building department, contacted concrete companies, and did her magic on getting great prices and quality work.

When the congregation was told at the next service about the new activity happening at the construction site of the church and what was needed for the room addition for the preacher, the amount ***plus more*** showed up in the Building Fund that very same night. I guess Little Barb knew what she was talking about! The funding did indeed come through when needed.

Room addition underway!

Within the next couple of weeks, the slab was poured and we waited a couple of more weeks for the concrete to set thoroughly. We then started making the repairs to the end walls and started the framing of the new room addition at the rear of the building.

I hesitated to help too much on the building, because I felt kind of hypocritical. I didn't really have a "faith," and I was dealing with a lot already. But then I got to thinking about the miracle of how it had happened for me to find this congregation—and the people had been nothing like what I assumed Gay church people to be. These people were truly devoted to their religious upbringings, but weren't able to attend church in safety because they had not been welcomed by mainstream churches. ***I think God is going to frown on that!***

Seeing them showing up for work days and contributing what they could helped me feel a lot better about helping them. For me to have a place to go on Saturdays was really a nice break. It really felt like God wanted me to build His new church. He was opening my eyes to see things that I didn't see before about the Gay community, and it was uplifting for me in my life.

Once I felt comfortable seeing the people truly committed, I felt ***I*** could commit. I then told Little Barb what I would be able to bring to the table and what I needed from her.

Don D and Little Barb measuring for the room addition.

I told Little Barb I would help with getting the building built, but I needed her commitment to be my right-hand coordinator. We would probably need to meet one or two times a week to review progress, planning, and materials needed. I didn't need to know anything about the money, but I needed to have the materials acquired as I requested them, and they needed to be at the site on Saturdays.

My commitment was I would show up at the site every Saturday. I would find out who could do what, and assign people to the tasks I had planned. I would then monitor how people were doing. If they were good, fine, if they needed help, I would help them.

I then told her I had an extremely important issue that could be a deal-breaker if the answer is no. I asked her, "Can I bring my Australian shepherd dog named Sheba to the job site for work days?" She said, "Definitely."

Sheba went everywhere I could take her with me. She was the

sweetest, most well-mannered dog ever, and she lived for Saturdays when we started going out. Once Sheba realized it was going to be every Saturday, she knew when it was Saturday and would jump on me in bed to wake me up in plenty of time to get ready and not be late. It was hilarious!

Sheba is resting from a hard day's work

Sheba would get so excited to see the site. I couldn't open the truck door fast enough. She typically ran to Whit first. He was very good with animals. He was a vet tech in his day job. He always had a "Good morning" hug waiting for Sheba, and then she made her rounds greeting everyone on the job. Usually, Al and Don D. were her next favorites to get her morning greetings from. Everyone just loved her.

Once we started working, Sheba would follow me around as I got people started or showed them how to do whatever they were working on. She would last for about two or three hours. After that, she would find her a spot outside the hot building where she could lie down and watch me no matter where I was in the building. She never lost sight of me and never got in anybody's way.

Once I started working with Little Barb coordinating work days, we started to get the front and rear walls repaired and started framing the addition. I put Whit and Sue on that project. They worked well together.

CHAPTER FIVE
CAN'T BUILD A CHURCH WITH FIFTEEN DOLLARS

Shortly after we had gotten the slab placed and started framing the office, I was on the building committee and would attend church service on occasion, to show face, and update people where we were on the building progress. This one particular evening, I was a bit upset about the pamphlet they handed out with the service program—it had a few items listed about the building contributions. I was sitting next to Little Barb, and I whispered, "How do I get to make a statement at the end of service?" She said, "The pastor will ask for comments. You can raise your hand, go up front, and say what you want to say."

So, I nodded my head and continued listening until the end of the service. When the time came, the pastor addressed a few things and then asked if anyone would like to make an announcement. I raised my hand and she called me up.

I got out of my seat and slowly walked up to the front with my pamphlet in hand. I stood there for a minute or so, very quiet, with my head down. Then, I lifted my head, looked around the church, looked down at the pamphlet in my hand, and opened it up. I then pointed to the part in the pamphlet that indicated how much money had been donated to the Building Fund the week before. "This pamphlet says that $15 was donated to the Building Fund last Sunday." I paused for a minute, then continued, "Do you know how much building material can be purchased with $15? None.

"I was called here by God to build this building with you, apparently for Him. I have tried to get out of doing it, but He keeps clearing the path to direct me back because that is what He wants me to do. I am also sure

you know you were called to provide the labor and money to build because you all found this place somehow, just like I did. You started this long before I came here.

"We've been getting a pretty good flow of volunteers in the short time I've been here, which is great. But we need more money than $15 donations to get the job done.

"I am meeting Little Barb, sometimes a couple of times a week, for planning and putting together a materials list for her to get and take them to the building—oftentimes by herself. This is over and above her 40-hour-a-week job. Little Barb is not charging the church one penny, and neither is Big Barb, who often gets materials on work days when we find we need something. She also brings lunch and drinks for the workers.

"Everyone who comes out on work days are unpaid volunteers. Little Barb and I have a goal to get this building completed in about one and a half years. This isn't an official date, but just a goal we feel is realistic. But if we don't have the money flowing all the time and the labor showing up regularly, we won't be able to reach that goal.

"To reach this goal, one of the primary tasks that has to be met is that this $15 figure needs at least two or three zeros after it every week! I know a lot of people can't work out there or contribute much money, but how about coordinating with Big Barb to spread out the work of taking on providing lunches for the crews one day a month? That would be a huge help. You can even work with two or three people to make the job easier and cost less for each of you—and it will be a great time of fellowship.

"You don't have to know anything about construction. I have many jobs that can be done by almost anyone. Come talk to me if you want to help even if you don't think you can. We can also use people to come out and work on the grounds of the property. There is always a need in that realm!"

That evening, the building fund raised over $2,000—and did consistently for a long while.

David just recently told me, while writing this book, that after my announcement about the finances that needed to come forward, he and several other members of the church got together and discussed what needed to happen financially to get the church built. All of it was now underway at full speed. The framing was going to be happening, then the wiring and insulation, drywalling, windows, doors and so on —and it couldn't be done in parts. It had to flow steadily.

At the next work day, when there was no money to buy supplies for the next workday, the Barbs gathered five or six of the members together and sat at a picnic table by the trailer and discussed the need for more funds to be able to provide the materials needed for each work day.

All of them actually started cleaning out their saving accounts and retirement accounts. Now, that is true dedication, faith, and love for your God and knowing that you are responding to a mission from God!

Drying in the roof of the room addition because we have money again!

With everyone pulling together, they came up with $15,000 for the Building Fund so Little Barb could purchase the materials on my building list as needed without any concerns of not being able to keep moving.

Little Barb and I met pretty regularly, making plans for the work to be completed the following work day. That woman was some kind of special. She was a genius in her career and she was just as much a genius in getting the best bang for our buck.

CHAPTER SIX

THE IMPACT OF THE BARBS AND DECEMBER 1, 1991 IS CHOSEN FOR THE DATE OF THE FIRST SERVICE

Every week, Little Barb would take my materials list to Lowes and get a written quote for the materials. She would then go across the street to Home Depot to get a quote from them, because they always advertised that they would beat Lowes by 10%. She would then take the quote from Home Depot to Lowes and get a quote from them that was 10% less than that! Then, she'd pay for the materials and have them loaded into her truck.

Big Barb and Little Barb were extremely devoted to the church

Little Barb would bring the materials to the site. There is always something that you forget, so we needed a "go-fer." She and Big Barb came to a decision between the two of them that Big Barb would stay home during the morning, waiting for Little Barb to call her and see if we needed more materials. She would then go to the store that gave us the best price and we would unload her vehicle when she returned to the site.

I learned about how the Barbs worked this agreement out themselves. I didn't even know about it until 32 years later, when I interviewed David for this book.

Big Barb socializing with the workers on a day she came with lunch.

Little Barb and Big Barb were devoted to the church and were there every work day. Big Barb couldn't do much of the manual labor work, but she helped with the books for the church and she brought drinks and food for lunch.

As our work force started getting bigger, she recruited more members to prepare food for us. We would have homemade lunches every day. The Barbs truly were major motivators to keep people excited about the progress, money flowing in, and labor showing up every week to make the project even more fun. These volunteers were so happy to be able to participate in the building of the church. They were typically older women or men who couldn't physically do anything on the building, but they knew we really appreciated their contributions.

Typical lunch table set up.

Lunch was one of the best parts of this project. The mobile home on the property was brought in to be an office and storage room. We would set up six-foot-long tables for lunch, and everyone would go into the air-conditioned mobile home to enjoy lunch out of the big steel quonset hut building, which felt like an oven on hot days.

Lunch was always so much fun. We would laugh the whole time! Construction was new to everyone that was working there, so there were always stories about what they were doing and how they would have never thought they would do something like this or were surprised they ***could*** do this kind of stuff. We got to know each other as truly part of a family during the work, and even more when we would break bread together and share experiences and jokes.

After about an hour, we would get up and get back to work, and the cooks would take the bowls and leftovers home. It was so awesome working with such a great group of people who were there for one goal, and that was to build this church.

Six months or so into working weekends on this project and brainstorming with Little Barb on several occasions, I hadn't yet figured out all the details of how we were going to frame the walls to enable us to maintain the curve and bend the drywall to match the shape, but we were getting closer and getting a lot of things done—and we were getting more people to show up on a regular basis.

Enjoying lunch!

In the Fall of 1990, we had been working on the building for almost half a year. The crew and I got to talking around the lunch table. Did I think it might be possible to finish in time for Christmas next year? I said, "Well, if we can keep the people coming and money flowing, it could be doable." With that, David just threw out the date of December 1, 1991 as our target to have our first service in the new building.

You know when someone throws a number at you that is about 12 months away, you don't really think about it only being four work days during each of those months, making your actual time on the job only 48 actual work days with an unpredictable number of people actually showing up to work. It looks a whole lot different when you think about it later. That's when you say to yourself, "Judy, that is actually only about two months of work time, not 12 months. What were you thinking?" And you reply to yourself, "I don't know, but it's going to be okay. It will be what it will be."

The primary church workers supported that date, and we took it to the building committee and the pastor. We really just wanted to be in there in time to celebrate Christmas in the building that so many people had worked so hard and long for. How wonderful it would be at Christmas!

Sue and Whit had gotten the room addition and rafters framed in.

I had Whit, David, and Don D. put the sheathing on the roof and the exterior walls of the room addition. David and Don D. were tall men and able to hand the plywood up to Whit on the roof and helped him to shift the panels into place. They would then lift the panels to the exterior walls of the room addition and hold them up for Whit to nail them off. The three of them worked very well together getting it sheathed off.

Meanwhile, I had Sue and Little Barb frame up a four-foot-tall knee wall around all the walls in all the rooms inside the church. This was going to act as a base for the drywall and provide a cavity to get electrical wiring and insulation behind the drywall in those areas. They all worked together as a good team.

All this time working on the church building, I was still working for the nonprofit, NHS, that I had started with in 1989. I was grateful for this job and enjoyed it very much. Unfortunately, one day, in June 1991, the executive director went to the bank, withdrew all of NHS's money from the account, got herself a new sports car, packed a bag, and left her husband, the non-profit, and Gainesville in the dust. This was not expected, and it was only seven months before the December 1 deadline.

There had been five employees in this organization, and to this day none of us know what happened to the director. All we knew was that the money was gone, she was gone, and we had 10 families that had been relocated from their homes, all in different stages of reconstruction. We had no money to complete them, and all five of us employees were out of a job. The next week we were trying to figure out how to save the organization, but she had really burned the trail and it was a real mess. After four days, we had to call it quits and shut the doors.

We did get unemployment benefits, but that wasn't enough to pay the mortgage and bills, so I knew I would need to spend my time looking for a job, not advising for and building a church for free. I needed a job. I was not looking forward to having to tell Little Barb I wouldn't be able to work on the church any longer.

I went ahead and worked the next workday so I could tell Little

Barb what happened and that I would probably need to cut back working on the church for a while.

CHAPTER SEVEN

MIRACLE #2: I DREAM OF HOW TO FASTEN THE FRAMING AND BEND DRYWALL ON A CURVED WALL MIRACLE #3: THE CONGREGATION HELPS ME FIND WORK

The next workday turned out to be another day of making good progress. I was going through the building, putting the materials list together for what would be needed for the next work day, ***when I noticed a box in one of the closets. In the box, were hundreds of thick-gauged 16-inch long, 1 1/2-inch wide straps that I had never seen before.***

I asked Little Barb where they came from, and she responded, "They came with the building and were used to tie the building to the footing bolts." I was surprised I had never seen them before, and it ran through my mind to remember them because we could possibly use them when it came time to frame the ductwork chase.

By now, everyone had cleaned up and left the site. I took this opportunity to talk to Little Barb. I explained what had happened with my job and that I might need to step back a bit until I could get another job. I told her I would be there for workdays as long as I could, but that I might only be able to meet up on workdays because of the cost of gas and I would keep her up to date. I also told her the plan for the next workday and gave her the materials list.

She was understanding and sorry about what was happening, and was praying for it to resolve itself soon. Then, she asked me to come to church the next day. I didn't know why she wanted me to come, but I agreed to.

That night is when I feel Miracle # 2 happened. A dream came to me that night showing me exactly how I needed to build the wall system. It would take care of all the things that had to be installed to handle every aspect of this whole system. It ran in my mind like a movie, and it actually stayed in my mind into the morning.

I normally don't wake up during or after a dream and remember it, but this one really stayed with me! I got up and immediately got a pen and paper to draw it up so I wouldn't forget it—and to also show Little Barb. The real interesting part of the dream was that the straps I found the day before were the missing link I needed to be able to build the framework grid to follow the shape of the arch exactly.

I called Little Barb during the next day after I had drawn up a set of drawings for her to submit to the engineer to get them stamped. When I talked to her, I told her the answer had come to me in a dream and would work like a charm. She then invited me to her house for dinner, so I went over. She was just as blown away as I was by how simple it was going to be to construct and how it tied everything together for exactly what we needed.

The next evening, after having dinner with the Barbs, I went to the church. At the end of the service, there was going to be an announcement by Little Barb. I figured that was what she wanted me to hear and why she wanted me there, so I stayed through the whole service.

At the end of the service, Little Barb got up and made the announcement. "We have made more progress in the last year or so on the construction of the building than we have in the two years prior. And I want to thank Judy for that." She also said, "I want to make you aware that the company she worked for went out of business this week, so she may not be able to help us anymore until she finds another job.

"So tonight, I would like everyone to say a prayer for Judy in helping her find a job so she can continue paying her bills and working with us." I was very touched by that, because no one had ever done anything like that for me before then. I thanked her when she finished, and we closed the service for the night with a normal prayer, plus a prayer thrown in for me.

As I was leaving, people started wishing me good luck on the job search. One of the women asked me if I could replace the rotten wood from around the base of her chimney stack, and then another person came up and asked me if I could do a good job painting the exterior of a house, and before I left that evening I had three jobs to look at—and more kept trickling in.

As it turns out, when I thought I was going to have to stop working on the church, the congregation helped keep me busy doing minor repairs around their homes. This enabled me to continue working on the church. I felt this was another one of God's miracles (#3) in this journey. God made sure his church was going to be built! ***He saw to it that I'd be supported.***

Little did I know there was even more to come!

Two months after NHS went out of business, the City of Gainesville determined they were going to take over finishing the projects that NHS had started. I got a call from the city Community Development Block Grant Department (CDBG). They asked me to come in and discuss a job possibility. They wanted me to come work as a temporary employee to complete the 10 projects that I had been working on for NHS. We worked out the details for a 20-hour-per-week job, and I started the following Monday.

I worked as a temp for the city for about six months to complete these projects, and they were so happy with my work that the City of Gainesville Housing Department asked me if I wanted to work as a permanent employee for the city. It was the same job I had already been doing, so they just made it permanent. I accepted the job and worked for the city for 16 years until the Obama era cut funds for the program. That was a tough pill to take, because I really enjoyed that job.

CHAPTER EIGHT
WE INSTALL THE STRAPS, MORE PEOPLE SHOW UP & MIRACLE #4: DAD SHOWS UP OUT OF THE BLUE

The next weekday, Little Barb took the drawings to the engineer, and they were approved. She then took them to the building department to attach them to the drawings. The next work day, she and I experimented on the best way to make this work—finally, we figured out that we could create an assembly line of people to get this built quickly and efficiently.

We decided we would announce in church the next Sunday to let people know we would need a few more people to help make an assembly line for the next phase, and that much of the work would be very easy to do and the volunteers would be able to sit a lot. We also took into account the summer heat in Florida. We had the A/C running in the mobile home-slash-office space so people could go in to cool off and rest, and when they were ready, they could go out and start working again. This way, someone could come in and replace another person if need be.

After the service, one of the women, Susan, a longtime member of the congregation, came up to me and said, "I am so glad that there is something that I can possibly do." Susan was an older large woman with many medical issues and contributed to the lunches on occasion, but she had always wanted to be hands-on with the building somehow. When she heard there were jobs where she could sit, she told me she was going to be there! Still, she asked "If I can't do it for very long, can I leave?" I told her, "Absolutely! We don't want anyone getting sick or hurt, and if you don't feel able to come in, then don't. We will understand. Also, God knows what you did and where your heart is, and that is all that matters."

I had Don D. and Al help me set up a table for the fabricators (strap benders) and chairs for four people close to the middle of the room. We also had fans blowing all over the place for all the volunteers working in the building.

Well, that morning, Susan showed up, and I set her up as one of the fabricators. Even though she was sweating profusely, she kept going. We had a fan on the two fabricators and enough water for everyone to drink. Susan was determined to stay as long as she could. She stayed until lunch, ate with us, and then left. She did great.

That work day, we also had approximately six extra people, including Susan, coming in at different times of the day. It was perfect. Many of them had never been out there before, and Little Barb and I were very happy to see the new faces. We had some elderly and disabled women and men show up, but all these people could do sit-down jobs, and that was primarily what we needed. We also had a few who were able to hand things to people up on ladders and to get water for them. If they needed to rest for a few minutes, they could.

Introducing Dad to the church.

Out of the blue, Miracle #4 showed up. My dad just walked into the building which he had never been to before because my mom would not let him. It was killing him to not be able to be a part of such a project and he told me then "I was not going to miss this for nothing in the world!" I was totally surprised to see him, especially considering how both he and Mom reacted to finding out that I was building a Gay church. Mom asked, "Of all the things you could build, why are you building a Gay church?" I said, "Well, I am Gay!" She and Dad were not happy and told me to leave.

That's basically when I came out to Dad and Mom. After about six months, Dad called me to apologize, but Mom and I never really had much to say to each other afterwards. There had been quite a bit of tension within the family since that day so you can kind of see why I was shocked for him coming today, but it was a welcome surprise and I was pleased to have the extra help!

We had set up two vise tables, each for a fabricator set to bend the metal straps that we needed made for the walls. Using a vise table, I made two prototypes of what shape we needed the fabricators to make. I then showed the fabricators what they were making, and then everybody got to it.

The straps created a way to frame up against the steel wall with 2×4s and then 1x4s that allowed us to bend and hang the drywall without compromising the steel building.

Everyone who would be fastening them to the wall needed

instruction, so I provided that, as well. I also made sure they all had their aprons filled with the steel nuts and a ratchet tool with a socket that Little Barb had purchased for this project.

I had four strap installers on each side of the building fastening the straps to the wall. As they had a few straps fastened to the wall, they would install a 2×4 into the strap to create the main framing along the wall. They were set up all over the floor area of the building areas to cover as much of the walls as efficiently as possible. I had Al working the wall areas over the kitchen and bathrooms. I knew he didn't really care for working on a little ladder, but he was fine working on a solid floor area. That was fine by me because it all had to be done.

When the fabricators had made a half dozen or so, the runners, and Dad, would take them to the installers. The flow of the assembly line was working perfectly. The plan was working, just like it had in my dream. By the end of the second work day, we had all the curved walls framed to receive the insulation and electrical wiring. This created a frame up against the steel building with 2×4s that enabled us to create a frame without compromising the steel building.

After the straps were put up and the framing was going up, Dad started showing up more often to help. He was really enjoying working with us and meeting all the new people. He was a hoot at lunch. He definitely enjoyed himself and he felt wanted and needed. He and I started making a stronger relationship, which was nice, and he started looking at Gay people more positively.

The purpose of bending the heavy-duty straps was to create an "S" shape of the straps and to bolt them to the extra length of the bolts that held the steel exterior wall together. With these in place, we had created a cradle for placing 2×4s perpendicular to the floor, at two feet apart, all the way from front to rear of the building and all meeting at the middle of the arch. This was the primary framing for the curved walls. It was a beautiful design.

This was the primary framing for the curved walls. It was a beautiful design.

The next work day, we were bending 1×4s and attaching them to the face of the 2×4s, which were also two feet apart, framing from the top of the knee wall we had constructed previously to the middle of the arch on both sides of the building. This was the part of the framing grid that would enable us to bend the drywall easily and smoothly. It would also make it easier for the drywallers to attach the sheets up onto a 3 1/4-inch face of the 1×4 instead of just the narrow edge of a 2×4. When everyone showed up, there were stacks of 1×4s. Many of the same runners showed up to hand these boards to the installers.

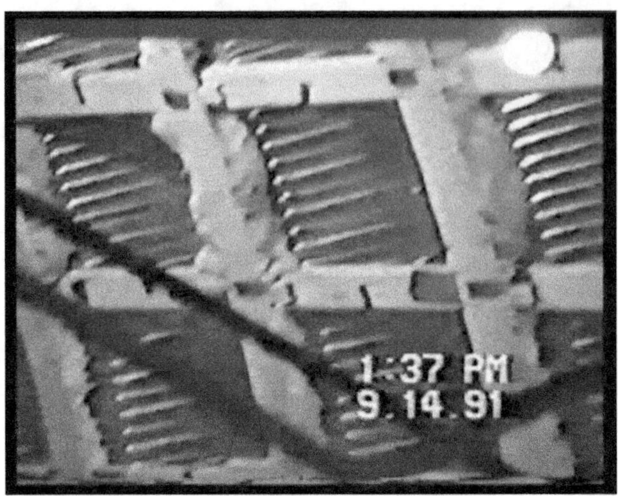

We were now able to insulate and wire behind the framework without having to cut any of the framing.

With this project, there were two people working together. They were placing the 1×4 board up to the 2×4 board. One person would push the 1×4 board into place up against the 2×4 board, and the installer would screw the 1×4 board onto the 2×4 grid. With this design complete, we were now able to insulate behind the framework and run the electrical wiring behind the 2×4s or 1×4s, without having to cut any of the framing. We were able to complete this task in two work days.

Little Barb and I designed the framing for the ductwork chase and the false beams for the light fixtures that would hang over the congregation. Little Barb and I put together the materials list for the remaining walls, the ceiling ductwork framing, and the false beams.

On the next work day, I asked Little Barb and Don D. if they felt comfortable working in the ceiling on the scaffolding to finish the frame work for the curved walls and then to construct the ductwork chase and false beams for the hanging light fixtures. I had concerns about Little Barb and Don D. working together on the scaffolding, because it was so hot in the ceiling and they were both in their 40s, or more. Neither one had an issue with the height difference or with working up there or being together. It worked out well because they were constructing the stability of the framing, which gave them something strong to hang on to.

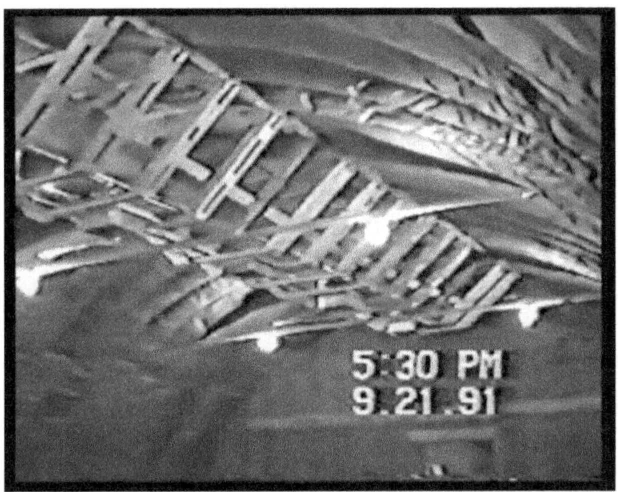

The ductwork chase, false beams, and curved walls insulated.

I had two other people on the ground to keep them hydrated, get them whatever tools or screws or anything else they might have needed, and help them move the scaffolding smoothly. They could adjust the fan onto them as they moved from one spot to the next. While they were on that scaffolding, they were pushing the insulation behind the 1×4s that had been installed over the 2×4 grid for the drywall. This design allowed the wiring to be installed concealed and safely prevent any accidental punctures from screwing into the drywall.

I felt for both of them up there! They were sweating so profusely that their shirts were literally soaking wet, to the point that they would drip water onto the floor below them. We couldn't get the towels to dry fast enough to be able to dry themselves once in a while, but neither one ever complained, not once.

I was the sawyer on the ground for them to construct and install the framework of the A/C ductwork and the false beams for the hanging light fixtures—and also for the crews installing the 1×4s on the walls. It took them two work days to get this project completed. It looked beautiful and worked perfectly for the curving of the walls, the A/C ductwork, and the wiring for the lighting.

At the end of this work day, all the framing was completed—even the ductwork chase was installed. Al heard me talking with Little Barb about the electrician and A/C contractors coming in the next week or so, after the framing inspection was passed, to do the rough-in and install the ductwork in the chase, so he came over and asked when they would be done. I told him "About three weeks. But don't worry, there's still plenty to be done beforehand and afterward."

CHAPTER NINE
WE GET THE FRAMING AND INSPECTION COMPLETED

As everyone was packing up to go, I asked Little Barb to call for the framing inspection and tell me when and what day they would do it on. I would need to be there to walk him through and talk to him if we needed to make any changes before we called in the electrician and A/C contractors.

I asked David if he could meet with me the day of the inspection, because I felt he was a better representative of the church. I thought that it would be good for him to meet the inspector. The inspector came and signed off on the inspection. This included the room addition and the replacement of the bottom plate to be pressure treated on the front and rear walls of the main building.

While David and I were there, I asked him to help me measure for how much insulation we would need to get for the rest of the building after the electrician rough-in was done and the A/C ductwork was installed in the chase.

I called Little Barb to let her know we passed the framing inspection and how much insulation we needed for a future upcoming work day. Then I asked her to call the electrician and A/C contractor we had selected and get them scheduled, hopefully, no later than the week after next.

With this part of the work completed and inspected, we were able to bring in the electrical contractor and the A/C contractor to get their rough-ins completed. This would include installing the ductwork in the chase, which would not be accessible after the drywall was installed. Once the drywall was installed in the A/C closet, we would be able to set the units and provide power to them to enable us to work in the building with A/C for the first time. That would be a day to celebrate!

The insulators are here!

Once we got the electrician and A/C contractors to come in and rough-in their parts, we had them inspected and were then able to insulate the ceilings and walls. The following workday Little Barb, already having the materials list in hand, had the site ready for the crew to learn how to install the insulation.

Even though we had gotten this far, with the framing and rough-ins completed, the final step before we could install the drywall was to install the insulation and have it inspected.

During this whole process, Whit would come to me at the end of every work day and tell me, "We are never going to be able to bend sheetrock in a curve. It's impossible!" I would always respond, "Just hide and watch. We will make that drywall bend."He always had a great positive attitude that leaned toward a negative thought. He was awesome, but difficult at times.

Well, the next work day came, and there were about 50 rolls of insulation in the middle of the room, plus two sets of scaffolding.

Little Barb hanging insulation on the curved walls.

I saw Al walk in, and said "Oh good, the insulators are here." He looked at me. "We are the insulators?" I said "Yep, today some of you are insulators, some are scaffolding pushers, and others are insulation cutters." They learned really quick they didn't like insulating because it's itchy, but they never complained.

I had Al focus on insulating over the kitchen and bathrooms because they had the solid walking area. I wanted the bathrooms done first, though, because that was where the air handler units were going to be located. That wall area would be priority when drywalling started, so we could get the A/C contractor in as soon as that area was completed. It took two work days to get everything insulated, but as we went, people were already feeling the difference in the temperature of the building.

At the end of the work day, Al asked me, "So who comes in next, after we're done with the insulation?" I told him the drywallers would be coming in the week after we got the insulation inspection. We were set to get the insulation inspected the week after next. As soon as that was done, the drywallers would be there.

The insulation was inspected and passed!

CHAPTER TEN
MIRACLE #5: TIME TO BEND SHEETROCK

The morning of our workday to start hanging the sheetrock on the curved walls, I woke up with a monster sinus infection. It was all I could do to get to the church. I wasn't going to be able to do much physically, but I was not going to miss this day for all the money in the world. I didn't know how long I was going to last for the day, but I knew if I got them rolling, there were enough of them that, over time, had learned plenty to be able to keep it going for the day.

Teacher Dad and students watching the miracle of bending sheetrock!

When I got there, there were two piles of sheetrock about five feet tall and two eight-foot tall stacks of scaffolding, one of each on each side of the building. When everyone started showing up, I told them right up front that I could not be up on the scaffold because I was sick as a dog, but was going to show them what they were going to be doing from the ground.

At this point, I pointed at Whit and said, "Whit, this is the day you are going to witness a MIRACLE! You will make drywall bend onto a curved wall."

I put Dad as the leader on the left of the building and Don D. as the team leader for the right-side. They kind of made a fun little competition of who would finish first, but I told them, "Just don't get too fast and get dangerous"—and they didn't. They just had fun! I was holding down the drywall on the right side in a prone position, and yelling out instructions to all the ground people and scaffolding people from my drywall bed. Like Dad, I wasn't going to miss this day unless I was dead.

Me on my drywall bed with the 4 ft knee wall in the background!

As bad as I felt physically, I had never been so proud to see a bunch of people with the courage to take on such a project without having a clue what they were doing. Talk about a leap of faith!

I was so honored to have been called by God to participate in the project. I was also happily surprised that I learned all my thoughts about all churches were incorrect, and that these people had blindly trusted this 25 year old stranger because of their faith.

I SOMETIMES WONDER IF I WAS CALLED TO HELP *THEM,* OR IF I WAS CALLED TO DO THIS PROJECT BECAUSE I NEEDED *THEM* TO HELP *ME.* EITHER WAY, BECAUSE I FINALLY SURRENDERED TO GOD'S CALL, IT WAS ONE OF THE BEST THINGS THAT EVER HAPPENED IN MY LIFE!

The four-foot knee wall at the bottom of the curved wall we had constructed earlier served two purposes. First, it was aesthetically attractive. Second, it acted as the bottom support of the bottom of the first piece of drywall. The top of the first piece of drywall was to act as the base for the bottom of the second sheet of drywall. This would enable them to push the drywall into the curve of the wall.

We had four guys on each of the scaffoldings, two guys on the ground holding each scaffold, and two people handing a sheet up to the guys on the scaffolding. They had to maneuver carefully so as to not knock anybody off the scaffolding, so when they got it into place, two of the ones on the scaffolding would push it into the wall with their backs and butts to fit into the curve of the wall. The other two would get several screws into the sheetrock so that another one could help him and give the others a break from pushing and get ready for the next sheet.

Al pushing the drywall to be screwed into place.

Al waving, "We did it!"

Men at Work!

By the end of the day, all the curved walls were now drywalled and ready to be plastered. We would still be hanging sheetrock the following two weekends, since we still had the kitchen, two bathrooms, room addition, a closet over the kitchen, and the A/C unit closet over the bathrooms. But the hard walls were done, and we were able to get the rest completed in a work day or two. Everyone looked at the walls and were just amazed that it had all worked.

Whit came over to me and said, "I have to admit, I didn't think it was going to work. But it looks great!" And I responded, "I didn't ever expect to hear you say that. Thank you. But it wouldn't have worked without all of these people here today and having faith. So thank you to everybody!"

Al came over next, and guess what his question was at the end of the day. He asked, "What happens next?" I told him, "Next week you guys will be doing the rest of the areas that haven't been drywalled, and the A/C closets will be mudded. After that, the A/C units will be put in. The mudders will be coming in the following week to mud the joints and get it ready to be sanded." As the reader it's your guess to see who the mudders are!

The left side team of drywallers won, by the way...

CHAPTER ELEVEN
THE MEMORIAL TRAIL AND MINI MIRACLES

After lunch on this particular work day, Al came up to me and asked if he could talk to me. We went for a little walk around the property. He was telling me about some of the friends of the church that had passed and that he had a desire to create a memorial walking path around the property. He was interested in working to keep up with the maintenance of the property, as well. He didn't want me to think he didn't want to work on the building. If there were times that he would be more useful working on the building, he would work on the building.

I said, "I don't feel like you're trying to get out of working on the building. I'm aware that you're one of the primary people keeping the cleared areas mowed, and it seems you would enjoy doing work outside the building a little more often.

He said, "I would, but I will do whatever is needed for the building." I said, "I'm grateful for that, because you are irreplaceable. This project is for all members that are here, and it's supposed to be a special experience. I want to let people, especially the founding members of the church, do some things that are just as close to their heart as the building is."

Al replied, "I have been wanting to do this for some time, but I was going to wait until the building was done. I can envision the trail, and am thinking of making it a memorial trail with a memorial pedestal at the very start of it. It can have bronze plaques that people can buy in memory of a lost loved one. We can attach it to the pedestal, and they can always come and visit it and see that their person hasn't been forgotten. I know a lot of people have lost people to AIDS and just general natural deaths, but so many of our people don't have families because they were disowned when they came out to their families and friends. They found new families in this community."

I told him, "I think your idea would be a great and beautiful thing and would be a really special thing to have in the works in time for the first service that we just talked about being on December 1, 1991. We have five beautiful acres here that make a peaceful area for people to come to pray, give gratitude, reflect, or whatever peaceful moments they may feel they would get from here. I've been thinking that it would be nice to have a little natural walking trail around the property through the woods myself—and had you in mind to oversee this project if you're up for it. Maybe build a few benches for people to rest or reflect along the way."

I told him, "There also may be days when I get more volunteers than I have work lined up for. Then, I would even be able to hand some of them to you, if you would like help to do this project." He was very excited about that. He made sure to confirm that if he was needed on the building, he would be there. He was more than happy to start on the project.

The rest of the day he worked on his plan for the path.

His plan turned out to be a beautiful thing. He and his crews cleared a route that wound around the property and around the bigger trees. It started at the east side edge of the parking area and wrapped all the way around the property, staying about 30 feet or more from the property lines and ending at a water retention mound near the entrance of the building.

I tried to make sure he always had at least two people to work with him. One time, we got a call from the MCC in South Florida who asked us if we could use 17 volunteers to come up and help. I asked Al if he could use about eight of them, and he said he could. I told Little Barb I could use that many. Naturally, we invited them up with gratitude! Al put eight of them to good use, and I used the rest. It worked out really well for both of us.

Other people who also typically worked doing yard maintenance on the workdays wanted to participate in creating the path. There were a few little benches built and installed with special gardens planted around them. They even created a few small water gardens close to the church entrance.

Memorial Plaque

Al also built the marble-topped pedestal with bronze plaques. His first plaques were for the members that had already passed. He would maintain adding other plaques as others passed. He, unfortunately, had to add a plaque for his partner, Don D., about four years after completion of the building.

Later, my father even got a plaque on the pedestal. That was very touching for me because that showed me that the church people that he worked with appreciated what he did for them and that he had proven that he accepted them as being Gay and in a church of their own.

Over the years, it was determined the bronze plaques were high maintenance, so a different platform was constructed with wood, covered with corrugated steel, and the names have been painted on it. So far, 29 names are on it, but Whit and the Barbs' haven't been added, yet. We just lost Big Barb, Little Barb, and Whit during the writing of this book.

There has also been a Rainbow Bridge built to enter a small designated park area for anyone who wants to attach a memorial collar or statuettes for the animals that have passed from people's lives. It is a cute little area.

Pet memorial

Another member of the church was named Les. He would often come to work on the building. He participated in the framing of the room addition. He was retired, and he and his partner were moving out of state. Before they did, they built a little amphitheater stage along the trail with benches for people to sing, pray, or reflect.

For him to do this project, an old wooden stage that had been stored under a tarp for several years had to be removed. We didn't want to take a chance on someone getting hurt by it, so we uncovered it, broke it apart, and burned it, because it was a hazard. I helped with the project of moving the stage sections and separating them to make it easier to break them apart.

If anyone is familiar with the wooded areas of Florida, they can be very moist and buggy. We have these spiders called Banana Spiders which can grow to about four inches in size, or basically the size of the palm of your hand. When we moved these pieces, we stirred up quite a few bugs that had been living in this pile for some time. As we separated them, we would have to be careful about not walking into Banana Spiders' webs! They are not dangerous, but if you walk into a four inch spider and its web, it will make the biggest, toughest bad-ass dude squeal like a little baby.

Well, when we got all the panels shifted, I was looking at them and instructing the people who were going to start breaking them apart. I had been leaning over the panel to show them how to cut the plywood into smaller, more manageable pieces. As I stood up and my arm came down my side, I felt something prickly which I had already noticed once before, so I looked down to see what it was just thinking it was a stick or something. I saw this huge Banana Spider sitting on my hammer and tool belt. Well, normally I'm okay with spiders, unless they are the large version, catch me by surprise, or are on me. Startled to say the least, I started screaming to get it off me! It was good (and bad) that Whit happened to be right beside me. He looked over and saw it and—so nonchalantly—just reached over, cupped it in his hands, looked at me, and said "Oh God, you are such a femme after all." I responded, "Call me what you want, just take him into the woods! Thank you."

We all had a good laugh, and all the guys there said, "I would have screamed louder!" It was quite a funny moment. After that, I said, "Okay, everybody knows what you're doing. I'll be inside!"

Early in the construction of the building process, I met one member of the church named Phillip. He was born with a very rare spine disease and had been in a wheelchair his entire life. The odds of him living as long as he had was a miracle in itself, but he was still living and even had a part-time job. He loved the community of the church.

One evening after church, Phillip came up to me after service and said, "I wish I could come out and help in some way, but I think I would just be more in the way than helpful." I said, "Phillip, I am actually very glad you approached me today, because I have a special job that I have been wanting to talk to you about. We even have the handicap parking pad and ramp in place for you so you can get into the building without any problem."

He was very surprised that he had been thought about and specially considered and asked me whether I was serious. I told him, "If you come to the building next Saturday, anytime in the morning, I will have your work station set up. Trust me, it would be a highly appreciated and important job that has been needing to be addressed for a long time. It not being done has been making me crazy." He said with a great big smile on his face, "I will be there around 10 a.m." I responded, "Perfect! See you then!"

That next work day morning, I asked Don D. and Al to set up a table for Phillip and to put all the boxes and piles of loose screws and nails on it. Phillip showed up as he said he would and I took him to his table. I showed him that on the table were some piles of different sizes of screws and nails. Then, there were several boxes of different types and sizes of screws and nails.

At the end of a work day, the people would be so tired they would just drop their aprons on the table and leave for the night. On the next work day, they would pick up an apron and just dump the screws or nails out of the apron onto the table, so there was a huge pile of different screws and nails on the table. They would just get new fasteners out of the boxes depending on what they were working on each day.

Now, if I had enough people show up on a day and one of them was good with that task for a couple of hours, that was fine, but sometimes when we had lots of people working, it became a disaster pile.

I explained to him. "Your task is to separate all of the screws with like screws, and the same with the nails, and then put them in their correct boxes. I know you have extreme limitations, but you let me know you wanted to be a part of it, and for me this job is a very important job. So, it gives us both what we want. Are you okay with this task?" He responded, "This is perfect. I will be here every work day to do this as long as you need me." I smiled at him and said, "Perfect! Looking forward to working with you. Okay, the mushy stuff is over! Get to work." I gave him a wink and turned to see what was going on everywhere else, and he got to work.

He did show up for about six weekends, and then a miracle happened for him. If I got the story right, at some point in his life he had lost connection with his family and didn't learn of them for 40 years. During the construction of the church, he connected with his birth family for the first time. They came to meet him, and he found out he had brothers and sisters who had been looking for him but didn't know how to find him. He found out he had a different name and a large extended family! They were very accepting of his being Gay. They just wanted to be there for him. They flew him out to where much of the family lived. Everyone got to meet him, and it was just a great family reunion. He was very happy, and it changed his whole outlook on his life. He now had friends and family.

CHAPTER TWELVE
THE DEVIL IS IN THE DETAILS

We had made so much progress over the year I had been working with the people of this church. They were so grateful for what I had done to help them get their dream done, and I was grateful for the friendships and new family members I had gotten to meet and work with. It was a very special project to my heart, just as much as it was to theirs.

We were to the point where everyone was able to see that their dreams were actually going to come to fruition. They were very excited and motivated at this point, but I had to warn them that we still had a long way to go, so don't lose your momentum! Our first service date, December 1, 1991, was less than 10 months away—only 40 working days.

Hanging sheetrock in the pastor's office.

The next couple of work days were spent on hanging drywall in the ceilings and walls in the bathrooms, kitchen/storage room, and the room addition. I also got many started on doing the mudding on the curved walls.

Note: Mudding is really just my term. Many people call it plaster, but plaster is actually a completely different type of wall finish that goes way back in how houses used to be built. It is still used, but typically only on high-end homes. I will let you research it if you're interested in the details!

Dad teaching everybody to do the mud.

The true name for "mud" is called joint compound. It's a product that looks like white mud, and you buy it in five-gallon buckets. The reason I call it mud is because it is messy like mud. When you apply the mud to the joint of where the drywall joints meet, a four-inch wide fiberglass mesh is placed over the joint, and then you use a six-inch putty blade for the first coat. You let that coat dry and sand down the high spots, then come in with a ten-inch-wide putty blade to apply a second coat.

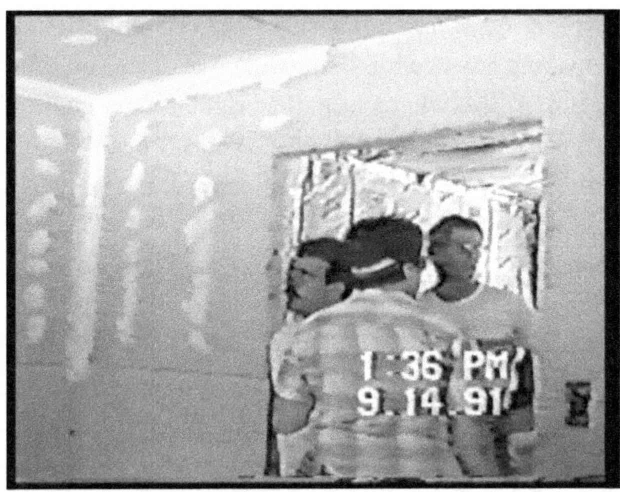

Students watching Dad and learning to mud.

When this is dry, the fun part has arrived. Now, you get a sanding pole and sandpaper and sand each coating of mud after it has dried. Every joint is sanded to make a smooth blend after each coat into the drywall. You want to wear goggles and a mask. The room gets very dusty, so you want fans blowing the dust out of the room. You're looking up for most of these two projects, so you're blind most of the time. Everything is aching, so you have to take lots of breaks.

We did have a few electric sanders, but they will vibrate your hands off, so you wind up switching hands about every five minutes. Needless to say, this is not the fun part of a construction project.

I don't know how many of you have heard the phrase, "The Devil is in the details." Basically, from this point to the end is when this phrase is best understood. Everything up to this point has been stuff that is invisible in the end—now the drywall, trim, flooring, cabinetry, paint, etc. are brought into the game. The rest is what people are going to be looking at for the next 20 or 30 years, with the exception of an occasional paint job or remodel. When you get to these final details you think, "Oh boy, we're almost there!" And then, as you're doing these projects, it doesn't seem like you are making any progress. They're the things that take the longest to install because you want them done right. As you're doing these projects and they don't seem like you're making any progress, suddenly one day…You're done!

Well, we aren't anywhere near that right now. It will take every one of those work days to get to the December 1 deadline, and we will still have other projects to button up afterward, but we ***will*** be able to use the building for the first service!

Today was the day everyone was going to learn how to apply the mud on the joints of the curved walls. Some did better than others, and many were afraid of whether they were applying enough or too much. So, I spent a lot of time that day going to everyone, and helping them work with the tools, and getting the mud in the joint and not messing up the mesh. They did a pretty good job for never having done it before. It is like trying to create a sculpture out of wet mud instead of chiseling it out of stone or a blob of clay on a spinning potter's wheel.

| ***Still plenty to do…tick tock, tick tock!***

I also spent time during this day in the A/C unit closet because I wanted to get the air handlers installed in that closet when the A/C contractor and electrician could come in together. That closet wouldn't need a second coat on the joints, because no one would be up there. I wanted the units installed soon so we could be working in a cooler environment and it would start acclimating the building and materials.

At the end of the day everyone was asking me, "Are you sure this is going to be okay? There are some pretty thick areas, and some just look really bad." I assured them the first coat of mudding never looks good, but it would be fine. The sanders would come in the following week, knock a lot of the high parts down, and smooth it to make it easier for them to do the second coat. "You'll see!"

The second work day of the drywall process was the sanding day for the first coat. Little Barb had gotten several packages of dust masks, sanding poles, and packages of sanding paper. She had brought her Shop-Vac from her house. Al looked at me and said, "This stuff is for the sanders coming in, right?" I replied,"Yes it is, and you got here just in time. Thanks for coming in this morning." He just rolled his eyes and walked toward the equipment.

While I was writing this book, David was a big help to me because he had been involved with the church from the very beginning. He's also one of the few who is still alive. We lost Whit in 2023. During one of our conversations about this book, David made the comment, "You always told us that the next subcontractor would be in the next week, and we just never got it that ***we were those subcontractors!*** It is just amazing how none of us ever put that together."

We both got a big laugh out of that.

So, I proceeded to show them how to put the paper on the poles and how to sand the now-dry mud. It was a little difficult in the beginning to get it knocked down because there were some rough areas. Fortunately, joint compound, once dry, is fairly easy to sand. We had about three people on each side of the building sanding, with fans blowing the dust out of the front openings. We had four or five people working on putting the first coat of mud in the rooms of the room addition, kitchen, and bathrooms.

I had Al over the kitchen sanding on that curved wall, and he was miserable. He couldn't stand the sound of the sandpaper on the walls. It was like fingernails on a chalkboard to him.

(For the younger people that may be reading this, chalkboards were used in our schools back in ancient times. The teacher would write on it with chalk instead of the dry-erase boards that are used now. They were obnoxious tools to use, but they were around for generations.)

I knew he was suffering, but he wouldn't give up. He even put something between his teeth, because it was causing him pain. After a little while, I climbed the ladder and went up to talk to him. "If you want to go work on the property, you can do that for a couple of our work days. It is not worth being in pain." He replied, "I told you I would work on the building when I was needed, and I am needed." I said, "And as I told you when we had that conversation, you are invaluable. But I want this whole thing to be a good experience for everyone, and this is not being a good experience for you right now. You were a huge help to get us to this point, and we have more people showing up now. They don't seem to be as affected as you are. So why don't you go get some happy on and go work on the property?"

He thought about it for a minute and said "Okay, I will finish this area, and then after lunch I'll work on the trail for a while." I responded, "As long as you're comfortable with that, that sounds like a plan. Thank you for your persistence and your always being here every work day. I love that about you and Don D. I'll let you get back to this and go stir up trouble elsewhere." We hugged and I went down and checked on everyone else.

The sanding was coming along well, and everyone was definitely ready for a lunch break. Everyone was talking at lunch about they had found muscles in their necks and upper body they had no idea they were there and they knew that they would be yelling at them tomorrow.

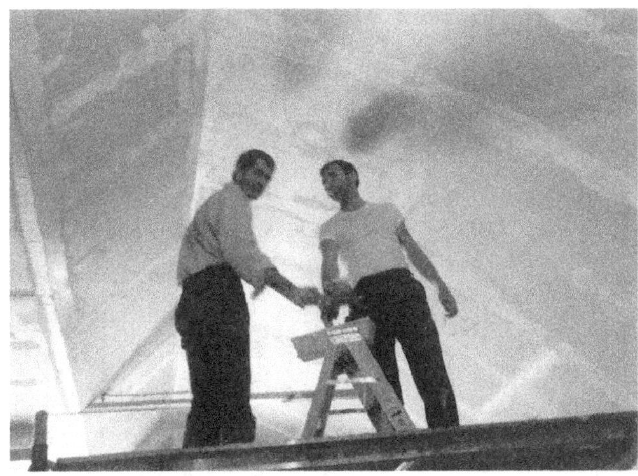

Don D. and Al mudding the second coat on the arch and the A/C duct chamber.

By the end of the day, the sanding was done in the main church area and the first coat of mud was looking good in the kitchen, bathrooms, and room addition. Before everyone left, I told them to just stop for a minute in the main church area and look around at how it was looking. "Did you ever think you were going to see this day? It has been how many years since this journey began? And today you have drywalled curved walls, and you guys did it all. Soak it in and be proud and humble that you were involved in such a miracle as this!"

I then let them know that the following week we would be putting the second coating of mud in the main church area and sanding all the other rooms that had been mudded that day. We were almost done with this awful part. "But we still have a way to go! So don't lose your momentum."

The next work day, we had another good showing of workers and were able to get the main church area second-coated and the other rooms sanded. I gave Al a couple of people to help him on the trail, because I was hoping he would have a good start on that before December 1. He was much happier working on that part but was ready to get back on the building to paint the inside when it was time.

While we had plenty of people working on the mudding and sanding, I had Don D. and Whit installing the metal roofing on the addition and adding ackempucky on all the bolts of the quonset hut building itself to ensure no leaks got into the building. Later, I put Don D. sanding inside the building and I had Little Barb, David, and Whit installing the cedar siding on the room addition and on the front wall, as well. We chose a metal roof because it would match the steel building better and would last for at least 50 years. The cedar planks went from the ground to the bottom of the metal building. It looked like it belonged in the forest, and the planks going up made it look like the trees.

Whit installed the ackempucky!

It was perfect.

Big window installed and siding getting going.

With the drywall and siding installed, we were able to install the windows and doors and have them trimmed out. We had large panes of tempered glass to install at the front entrance over the double doors and on each side and at each side of the room addition to enable the congregation to look at the woods during the services.

They were custom-made tinted tempered glass sections, and it was a very concerning project.

I was the one who actually installed all the doors and windows. I was the only one qualified to do it, and also if anything was going to go south, I wanted it to be on me and not somebody else feeling bad about it.

I had trimmed out the opening to receive the biggest window that was over the main entrance and then brought the pane up to put it in the opening. This pane was very heavy, so it was a lot of work getting it eight feet up into the air and into the opening. I had two people on the outside just for safety, not allowing the window to bind up anywhere—and one on each side of me to help lift it up and into the opening. I had Little Barb on the ground being my sawyer for cutting the trim pieces.

The rest of the windows were much easier to install. This made me very happy, because tempered glass cannot be cut or ground down to fit into an opening if you don't get the measurements right. Fortunately, we didn't have that problem on any of them. They all fit like a glove and came out looking great!

Before we started hanging sheetrock, I was looking at the wall over the area where the pastor would be speaking. It was just a wall all the way to the ceiling. To me, that would have just made for a boring wall. So, I talked to the primary people involved and asked them what they thought about cutting openings between the framing that just so happened to have the middle stud at the exact center of the wall.

All of the windows were sold by the end of the next service!

I suggested that we could put 10 14-by-14 inch windows up there. It would allow a little light to shine in and lighten the sermon area. Everybody liked the idea. Then, Al took it to the next level. He said,

"We have a member of the church who does stained glass. I'm sure I could talk him into coming up with some designs and offer them to people that would buy them as memorials for their lost family member. The stain glass cutter would only charge at cost and would allow us to charge a higher fee to donate to the church." Everyone was concerned the cost wouldn't go well with the congregation, but if they could all be sold, they would agree to that idea.

By September 1991, we had the building insulated, sheetrock installed and sanded, and the doors and windows installed. We had the exterior siding installed, and the A/C handlers were in place and up and running. We were in pretty good shape to be finished by December 1—but as I stated earlier, the "Devil is in the details."

About this time, Reverend Bigelow, the district coordinator, came to witness the building's status. If you remember, he was there to witness the lifting of the first arch. He was impressed with the progress that had been made and agreed "that, indeed, we were ready for the first service to be December 1, as planned."

I had Whit and David working on installing T1-11 plywood on the knee wall framing. Then, they covered it with plastic to keep dust or paint from getting onto the raw wood until we were able to seal it with the polyurethane. I didn't want to install it before now because it was to be stained, and I didn't want it to get scuffed up while doing the other major projects. We were going to do that when we had a work day with just a few people so there wouldn't be any people exposed to the fumes without masks. Now that all the walls were sanded and ready to be painted, we still had to get the bathrooms tiled and install the fixtures.

CHAPTER THIRTEEN
MIRACLES #6 AND #7: TILE AND LABOR FOR THE BATHROOMS

Out of nowhere, Miracles #6 and #7 called me on the phone. It was my dad on the other end! He told me he had just finished working on a little commercial job that had a lot of 4-by-4-inch ceramic tiles left over from the bathroom tilers. He was curious if we could use them at the church. I asked him how much he had, and he said over 50 boxes. He told me the owner didn't like the color, so he rejected the order and the supplier just replaced them with the color of his choice. So he gave all the rejected tile to Dad.

"They're a little different color," Dad said, "but it's a typical color for commercial buildings. It's like a pinkish purple." I said, "They sounded beautiful when you said they were ***free***!" He then said, "I have something else I was wondering if you would be interested in. I'm not going to be working in the field anymore. I can't do it anymore with the heat. But now that you have the air conditioning working at the church, your Mom and I would like to come out and install the tile in your bathrooms."

I just about swallowed my tongue when he said Mom wanted to help.

My mom had not set foot on the property since I started the project in early 1990. It was now 1991, and we still really hadn't spoken to each other very often since I came out.

While Dad and I had worked out an apology and terms of respect, my mom, however, was a different story. My entire life, she and I were always like two rams hitting head horns in battle, and I had no desire to even try to fix her problem.

To hear that my mom would be interested in working at the church that had been touched all over by Gay people was a shock. I confirmed with Dad that she didn't come around while the rest of us were working. I didn't want her judging anyone of anything. He agreed.

To make Dad's job easier, he wanted to do the tile work in the evenings so no one would be going in and potentially touching or stepping on tiles setting in wet mortar. Dad came out to the job site on a work day to get some people to help off-load the tile, mortar, and grout from his truck. He naturally had to walk through the building and check it out, and he was so happy to see the progress that had been made.

I was hoping that Dad and Mom were able to get the larger bathroom tiled, but I was surprised they got both bathrooms tiled around the first of November. After they finished the smaller bathroom tile work, Dad was trying to do the plumbing. He found that there was not a drain line for the toliet, but there was one for the sink.

To correct this problem, we were going to have to bust a hole in the floor big enough to get some small-bodied, fearless soul to tunnel over to the other toilet, cut into the pipe, put a "Y" into the main, and run a line to the second bathroom.

I had only one person that would be thrilled to receive this project and would consider it a special Christmas and New Year's gift. A week before the first service, about the middle of November, I asked Whit how he felt about doing it. He said "Why aren't we doing it yet?" Like I said in the beginning, he was fearless, and just crazy enough to enjoy doing this kind of thing.

I asked Little Barb to rent a concrete saw. "Also, make sure we have several masks for Whit, a ***big*** roll of Visqueen, and if you would, please bring your Shop Vac back." Concrete sawing is so dusty, but especially in a six-foot-by-eight-foot room.

We got Whit set up, basically hung plastic around the door to that room, and made a tunnel out the front door to keep the dust down in the main building. Everyone had to come into the building through the side door or room addition door.

Once Whit was done cutting, he took a break. I kept the fan going while he was taking a break. I had a couple of people start working once he got the concrete cut and broken up. They wheelbarrowed the pieces out to the woods, and we eventually made some garden areas around the woods. Whit then started scooping dirt out of the hole he cut with a handheld shovel. He would fill a five-gallon bucket with dirt, and his helper would move the dirt bucket to the kitchen/storage room and entry hall because that dirt had to go back into the hole.

Whit dug his hole to get to the other toliet.

Since Whit was making great progress on his hole, I went to check on everyone else. David was working on staining the exterior cedar siding on the room addition, along with a couple of others. He asked, "What's Whit up to? I haven't seen him for a while." I told him, "Whit is tunneling under the floor of the second bathroom to the big bathroom." He stopped what he was doing, looked at me and said, "What?"

I said, "He cut a hole in the floor and now he's taking the dirt out of the hole and tunneling to the big bathroom, because nobody put the toilet drain in the small bathroom." He said "Oh, I have to see that."

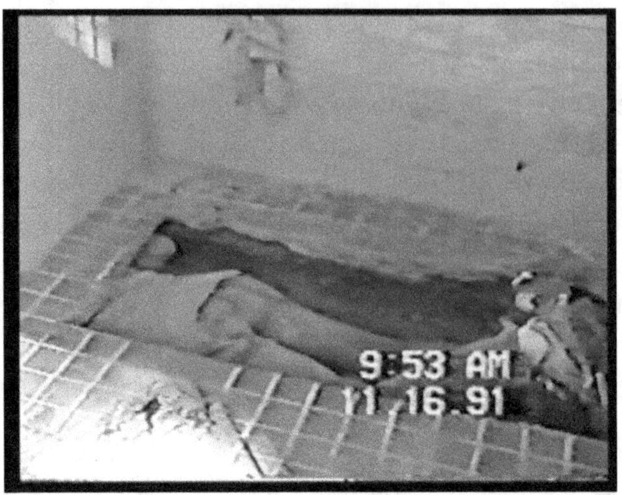

Whit going into his hole.

He put his stuff down, and we walked from the back of the building all the way to the front. He got to the bathroom door opening just in time for David to see Whit's little butt go under the floor.

He then said in his usual shocked-by-Whit voice, which was at least one octave higher than his normal voice, "Whit, what are you doing under the floor?" Whit called back, "I'm a little busy right now!" David looked at me and said, "I would never be able to do that, and just seeing him doing it makes me feel claustrophobic." He just looked back at the hole and said to Whit, "Be careful, and let me know when you're done." David just went back to his project on the room addition, and he never forgot it.

After Whit got to the other pipe, installed a new "Y" connection, and extended the pipe to the other bathroom, he then took the saved dirt and started packing it into the hole all the way to the other pipe. Then he got it ready to place concrete back into the floor hole. He got it all done, and it was dry in a week. Then, Dad came in and got the tiling done in that bathroom.

I was grateful that Mom and Dad were willing and able to get both the bathrooms tiled and ready by our first Christmas service. It was very generous of them to give us the free tile and labor. I think they appreciated the opportunity to work on my project and I appreciated that they came forward and did the work. It seemed that they both got a different perspective of their thoughts and ideas of what Gay people were like and at the end of it all, they felt like they contributed to God's mission, as well!

CHAPTER FOURTEEN
THE FIRST SERVICE IS INDEED HELD ON DECEMBER 1, 1991

Once November had showed up , we stopped working on the building and started getting it cleaned up to look good for the big day. We didn't have any flooring installed yet, but nobody cared since the floor was concrete. We rented 75 folding chairs for the service, and we filled almost every one of them.

The first service was indeed held on the morning of December 1, 1991, making it the very first morning service for the church, which made this an even more special event.

Whit leading the choir.

David held the service and discussed how pleased he was with how far the church had come and how many people had shown up. It was quite an emotional experience for all who attended. The people who came were so surprised and pleased to see the progress that had been made on the building because they hadn't seen it since the arches were all there was of the whole building.

David giving the first sermon in our church!

Little Barb had a backup plan!!

During the writing of this book, I learned that the day of the first service event we had not yet received our "official" Occupancy Permit. Little Barb was very nervous about this and was concerned about a building inspector coming by. So, as everyone was coming in, she would tell them to have a seat, but if an inspector showed up, they were to fold up their chair and take it to the woods. I guess her Marine Corps training was that they couldn't get us all! That's my girl!

Little Barb, the process documentary professional!

CHAPTER FIFTEEN
GETTING READY FOR THE FIRST CHRISTMAS SERVICE

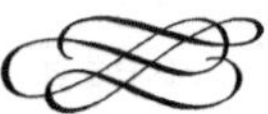

We were all thrilled with how the first service went. We knew that for many, the first service was the first time they had seen the building as anything more than a hollow metal building. It was now actually almost a completed church. It had been seven-plus years to get to this point, and many of the original 12 members were in attendance. That in itself had to create some emotions for some of the people who came.

Now, with the first Christmas service being just a couple of weeks away, we didn't want to get into anything major. We wanted to let people do their Christmas shopping and parties and visiting, so we kind of focused on short work days and wrapped up projects where we could.

Al's windows had been completed, and we installed them so we could enjoy them at the Christmas service.

Little Barb had built a podium for the new pastor that the board had just selected. He would be coming in the spring, but she wanted to bring the podium in so whoever was doing the Christmas service would have it if they liked one.

We were able to get the base cabinets set into place for the kitchen/storage room. We had planned on having a little covered-dish dessert gathering after the Christmas service, so they would come into good use for that.

Al was doing a lot to make sure the grounds were looking good for the Christmas service. He started using downed branches or trees that he had cut down to designate parking areas, because the parking area was mostly dirt except for the handicap parking pad. The Memorial Trail was looking really good, and people had been coming out and enjoying the serenity of it.

We were able to get the knee wall stained, and it looked really good. We didn't put the baseboard down right away because we hadn't put carpet down. We were still painting and didn't want to take any chances.

The week of Christmas Sunday, Little Barb went and rented 75 folding chairs again. We set up some of the six-foot tables at the back of the room, put some pretty red table cloths on them, and strung holly on the lighting beams in the ceiling. We had a big wreath on the front of the podium. We even had a baby Jesus in a stable scene set up on a table at the front wall. It looked pretty Christmasy.

It looked great and was very welcoming for the Christmas service. You wouldn't know that there was still a little more work to be done, but it was all aesthetic and wouldn't take but about three or four more work days, tops.

We had another great showing of church members for the first Christmas service. We had a new pastor coming in the spring, because our other one had left for personal reasons. David was the worship coordinator and Les was the assistant worship coordinator.

David gave a beautiful sermon that night, and it was truly moving. You could feel the Spirit in that building that night, for sure. As spiritually uplifting as the first service had been, the first Christmas service was even more special.

At the conclusion of this service, the worshippers exited the church, walked out past the front doors, and formed a circle. With lighted candles, we sang additional Christmas hymns and shared more fellowship. To this day, that tradition is still carried on.

What the church looked like between the December celebration and the Dedication Ceremony, when it officially became a church

After the first Christmas Service, we were that much more motivated to finish the building so we didn't have to keep decorating and un-decorating every week. We wanted to be done so we could officially move into our church and quit paying rent on the other one. Not that we weren't grateful, but we were ready to have our home completed and move into it.

The next work day, we started taking all the decorations down, boxing up what had been donated, and putting them into the storage closet over the kitchen. Our first official church assets—Yay!

After that, we just took whatever tools or things we weren't going to need anymore, moved most of them out of the room addition, and took them up to the mobile home. After the New Year, we could focus on finishing sanding and painting and completely finishing the building.

CHAPTER SIXTEEN
THE NIGHT BEFORE THE DEDICATION

In the next two months, everything was buttoned up and finished. We got all of the final inspections done and passed them all. Little Barb and Big Barb surprised everyone with buying carpet and having it installed in April, just before the arrival of our new pastor, for a formal dedication on May 17, 1992. We were actually able to buy chairs for the sanctuary and moved the desk and chair from the mobile home for the pastor's office along with a file cabinet to at least get him started. He could figure out what he wanted from there.

The new pastor arrived at the church a week before the dedication, and he received the final certificate from the building department.

Everyone wanted me to wear a dress to the ribbon-cutting at the dedication. I would always ask them, "When did you become my mom, and what is it about girls having to wear a dress to church?" I broke down and told them I would consider wearing one, only because I still had the dress I had from being a bridesmaid a couple of years before, and amazingly it still fit. It was still just as ugly to me, primarily because it was pink. I honestly believe it's a rule that all bridesmaids' dresses have to be ugly.

The night before the dedication, a group of us went to dinner at a popular Chinese restaurant in town. I had talked to a couple of the guys ahead of time and told them, "I don't really walk well in high heel shoes, so I need one of you to teach me." Immediately, Steve said, "Bring your shoes to the restaurant and I will teach you how to do it.

You'll be wanting to wear heels all the time after I'm done." I told him, "I just need to get through the event!"

That night, I wore knee-high hose, brought my shoes, and sure enough, Steve asked, "Did you bring your shoes?" I said, "Yes I did. I just hope I don't break my ankles!" We all laughed and ordered our food. After that, I took my tennis shoes off and put my heels on. Well, Steve started right off with how to properly stand up from a sitting position and then how to gently cross one foot in front of the other and if need be, hang your arms by your sides and just lift your hands to kind of balance yourself discreetly.

I asked him, "Will you please just kill me right now so I don't have to do this tomorrow?" He said," "Oh honey, if you only knew how beautiful you are and how smashing you'll look in a dress, but I bet you would also look fabulous in a tuxedo, as well!" I said, "Is it too late to rent a tux tonight? I would gladly have worn one of those tomorrow." After about 15 minutes of him walking with me, I felt much more confident, but still I had planned to change clothes shortly after the celebration.

I made "best man" look good!

As it turned out, about three months after the opening of the church, one of the members had a commitment ceremony, the closest thing to marriage a Gay couple could do back then. The bride was marrying someone new to the area and didn't know anyone, so she gave her bride the green light to pick whoever she wanted for whatever parts of the ceremony. She asked me to be one of the "best men" and told me where to get fitted for my tuxedo, and to tell them whose wedding it was for. I got a sharp pair of shoes—and I made that tuxedo look good! I know, because every Gay man in the building came up to me after the ceremony and told me that it was such a shame I wasn't a real man because I looked fantastic. You'd be amazed at how many straight girls made that same comment to me, as well, in my school yearbooks. I have many "Too bad you're not a boy" notes in those yearbooks. (My dream had finally come true.)

CHAPTER SEVENTEEN
THE MORNING OF THE DEDICATION AND MEETING THE NEW PASTOR

The morning of the dedication was a beautiful spring day. Before the event, I went to a costume store and found one of those Chippendale-type bow ties for my supervisor dog, "Sheba." If I had to dress up, so did she. So that morning, we loaded up and headed for the church. When we pulled up, you would have thought I was a movie star or someone famous, because literally everyone there came running to my truck with their cameras out and were taking pictures like crazy. It was like they were the paparazzi. I know there were at least 200 pictures taken of me that day. Everyone would say "Well, all we've seen you wear for almost two years has been a T-shirt and jeans with a tool belt and a hammer off your hip." I said, "I just hope you all know I feel like I'm in drag, so take your pictures and don't expect to ever see me this way again!" We all got a big laugh out of that.

The first pastor for our new church building was Pastor Jerry Seay, but he was the church's third pastor. The church members overwhelmingly voted for him and he accepted one week before the formal Dedication of the Building on May 17, 1992. Reverend Tom Bigelow officiated at the dedication, with Pastor Seay participating.

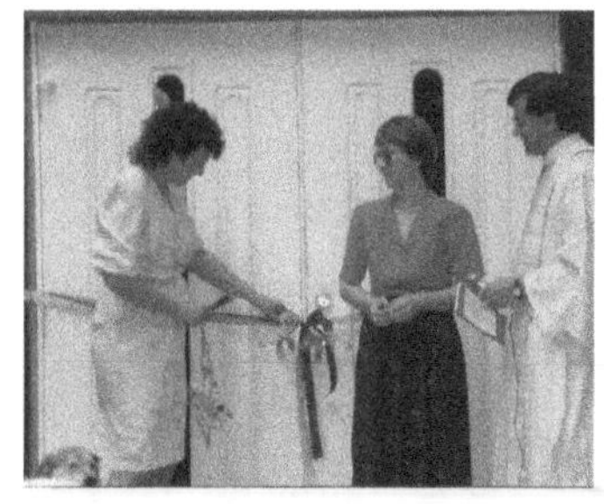

The ribbon cutting ceremony

During the celebration, Pastor Seay presented the building's Final Certificate of Occupancy (CO) to me. The CO is the document that proves the building was completed to the satisfaction of the state or county building department. Pastor Seay had accepted the certificate three days before the dedication, and the presentation was a major surprise to everyone—especially to me. I had not heard about the inspection being scheduled or that it had passed. I was very glad it did, and I was honored to have had it handed to me.

I accepted the CO from Pastor Seay at the church dedication May 17, 1992.

Jerry's arrival with his partner seemed to coincide with the city's debate over revising the county's civil rights legislation. Jerry was highly visible as the TMCC pastor. He was on TV, was quoted in the press, and stood up to conservative Christians who would use the Bible to condemn Gays and Lesbians.

Pastor Seay left after three years, 1995, and moved to Grace MCC, in Miami, Florida.

Dad was happy to be able to attend the celebration and he was very proud for the church. Unfortunately, he died six years later.

Les is painting the hands of all of the volunteers that participated in the construction of the church.

CHAPTER EIGHTEEN
GAINESVILLE'S FIRST GAY PRIDE MARCH

Once the church was officially open and we had a pastor in place, some old members started to come back and were quite impressed with how it turned out. One member, Cyndi, came to the dedication and to the service the following Sunday. She announced that the ***first official*** Gay Pride March in Gainesville would be on Wednesday, June 17, 1992, one month after the church's dedication. Part of the plan was to paint the entire wall on 34th Street pink, so they needed about 30 or 40 volunteers to come and help out. They just needed people. All the supplies would be provided.

The 34th Street wall is still there and is still an icon used by the students every new semester to paint their expressions or artwork. The paint layer on this wall was about two inches thick (back then) and the wall is about one and a half miles long. The police had tried for a while to stop people from painting on it, but after so many years it had become an icon of expression. Now they kind of look away if they see anyone doing anything on it, as long as it doesn't have any profanity.

The painting day was the weekend before the Pride March on June 17. We were to meet at the wall around 1 p.m. or when we could get there. About 40 people showed up, and we went through God only knows how many gallons of paint. I just know Cyndi had to keep going to the store to get more paint. By the end of the day, the whole wall had been painted, with the exception of the specially painted memorial piece of the five murder victims of Dan Rollins at UF in August of 1990. He became known as the "Gainesville Ripper." He slaughtered five college students, four women and one man, in four days. He was executed by way of lethal injection at the Florida State Prison in 2006. Nobody touches that area out of respect.

That was a very scary time for Gainesville.

Once the wall was done, I went down to both ends to look at it. ***It was an amazing sight to see and be a part of!*** The wall looked epic. One and a half miles of pink. I took pictures, but they have been lost over the years.

It was great timing, in that I had been working with a lot of people like me for the last couple of years and now I was stepping into another experience of getting to work with more people like me.

For the first time ever, we were going to gather and go public. It was a major historic event! There had to be 100 or more who showed up for the walk.

We walked from the University through downtown and ended at a plaza in the heart of downtown. We were all chanting the whole way down. A Gay owned T-shirt company made special T-shirts for us to wear. I still have mine.

We did have KKK members come out and try to threaten a couple of people, myself included, after the march, but we all anticipated it.

The KKK people followed a few of the people from the parade to their homes or rolled down their car windows to scream, “Faggots!” at us. They were just trying to keep the fear alive, but there were a lot of police cruising through town all day and night, and they must not have felt we were numerous enough to cause a problem. They didn’t stay around town for very long.

After the dedication and march, I continued going to the church for a while. I got a little involved with the community and got to enjoy going camping with Al and Don D., David and Whit and the Barbs on several occasions. Don D. had a condo on the beach, and many times we would go over there for the weekend, play in the ocean, and just enjoy the beach.

In 1993, ACT UP sponsored a march on the White House by Gay

people from all over the country. People from Florida went to Washington by busloads to show their solidarity.

David and several TMCC church members went to this rally. He recalls that when their bus stopped, they were by the Lincoln Memorial Reflecting Pool, between the Lincoln Memorial and the Washington Monument, when he noticed a younger guy sitting on the wall of the pool. David saw that the guy was holding a cardboard sign in front of him. It had "Washington DC" on one side and "Georgia" on the other side. This young person had hitchhiked all the way from Georgia and was prepared to hitchhike all the way back to Georgia when the rally was over.

David said the guy was just sitting on the wall with the biggest smile from ear to ear. He was just looking at all the people that had showed up. He just kept saying to himself, loud enough to be heard by others, "There are so many people here, and they're all like me!"

Can you imagine how huge a moment this event had to be for a young person from some small town in Georgia, where he probably had never met any other Gay person, or had lived very closeted? He couldn't tell anyone he was Queer because it could cost him his life, and now here he was in a crowd of a hundred thousand or more—All in one place, for the same reason.

CHAPTER NINETEEN
CATHERINE DEARLOVE BECOMES REVEREND OF TMCC

Reverend Catherine Dearlove came from Dorchester, Dorset in South West England. In 2010, she participated in a leadership retreat in Ellington, Florida. She enjoyed it so much, she knew she would be coming back.

Reverend Dearlove has been a member of MCC since 1982. She has a Bachelor of Theology from Brisbane College of Theology. She also completed a Masters in Contemporary Christian Spirituality at Sarum College, Salisbury. U.K.

| *Reverend Dearlove*

Reverend Dearlove joined Trinity Metropolitan Community Church in Gainesville, Florida. She is an ordained reverend and she has been at TMCC since 2015.

She has been quite visible as the reverend of TMCC in Gainesville, Florida.

She supported the community and the families of the victims after the devastating events that occured at The Pulse Nightclub in 2016 and Parkland School in 2018.

On June 12, 2016, a shooter went into a crowded Gay nightclub, The Pulse, located in Orlando, Florida, and killed 49 people and injured 58 others. The FBI called it a shooting of terror. The shooter was subsequently killed during a standoff with a SWAT team.

The Parkland shootings were on February 14, 2018 at the Marjory Stoneman Douglas High School in Parkland, Florida when a 19 year old shooter killed 17 students and injured 17 others. The shooter was sentenced to life in prison because the jury did not unanimously vote for the death penalty. He is still in the state prison in Raiford, Florida.

The Trinity Metropolitan Church website says Reverend Dearlove is known for her strong belief that "We can make the voice of love louder than hate!"

The Reverend's view from the alter

CHAPTER TWENTY
THE CHURCH'S FIRST FUNERAL: DON D

As an aside about Don D.'s passing four years later (1996), his death and funeral were quite difficult for me to handle. In the years after we had completed construction of the church, several of us from the construction group enjoyed going on trips together. One day, about a year before he died, I saw this horribly ugly, large raised mole on the back of his left calf. I told him it looked like something he should go see a doctor about, and he said, "I have seen the doctor already and he said it was ok." So I said, "Ok," but I wasn't really comfortable with that answer, but that was his business. Our group would go camping and on trips and dinners, and he never showed signs of feeling bad.

Then one afternoon, about a year later, Al called me to let me know that Don D. had had a seizure and was at the hospital. I went there to see him immediately.

When I got to the hospital, he had just had another one, but this one was a Grand Mal seizure. Al had just come in from work. I told him that I had seen that mole a year or so ago, but Don D. had blown it off. The doctor came in and told him that Don D. had a melanoma, and that it had spread to many parts of his body—including his brain. He told Al that Don D. didn't have much time left, so he needed to get his affairs in order while he had time being lucid. Al told the doctor that he had just gotten approved for a family leave from his job and planned to be there with Don D. from here until he was better.

The doctor said there was nothing they could do. His records showed that he had been made aware of this issue over two years prior and that he had told his doctor that he had no intentions of doing anything about it, nor did he want him to tell anybody about his condition. He said he would take care of his affairs and let God do what He plans. You could have blown Al and me over with a feather. I was a little surprised he hadn't told me a thing, but Al and I were both completely shocked that he hadn't told Al.

Al asked Don D. about this decision. He said, "I didn't want anyone to treat me differently. This was my fate from God because of what I am, and I accepted it." We didn't really understand what he meant by the last part of that comment, but we kind of put it together after his funeral.

Al told me he was on medical leave from his job for a month so he could stay with Don D. during the night, and asked if I would be able to on some days. He had other people lined up to come in, as well. I said, "Thank you for letting me be one of them to help. You let me know what days and times, and I am here. Since you are here for tonight, I'll go and let you be alone, and I'll see you and him tomorrow."

When I got home, my phone was ringing. I got to it just in time to hear Al on the other end crying really hard. I was trying to get him to tell me what had happened, and it took him a minute to be able to tell me. He said, "Don is gone." He had been talking to him and Don D. told him he was really scared of having another seizure. Just as they were talking, Don D. had another seizure, and was gone before any of the nurses or staff were able to get there. It just came on so fast, and then he was gone.

Al then asked if I could come over, and I said I'd be there in a few minutes. I only lived six blocks from this hospital. Al was just beside himself. I suppose I was too, because I am sure there was somebody else in the room— but I can't for the life of me remember who it was. More than likely David and Whit or Little Barb.

Most of us did not know much about Don D. He just kept his life to himself—even from Al, from what we found out after he died. Don D. was a professional at the University of Florida and had something to do with the livestock part of the veterinary school, but he never really talked about it. We knew that he was a real cowboy. He would be sent to Brazil every now and then to check their cattle and horses and other livestock, for whatever reason. He even told some of us he would testify as a professional witness in cases that he never really talked about. He was quite secretive in many ways—and for reasons more than that.

When Al planned the funeral for Don D., he knew Don D. worked with a lot of people at UF. He had worked there for over 25 years, so Al knew his co-workers would want to show their respect. The funeral was naturally at the church, but the church was going to be too small to handle the crowd. So Al had set up speakers and large TVs outside with lots of seating for the overflow.

All the church members were at the church, and then Don D.'s co-workers started trickling in. As I watched them coming in, it became obvious that they were very confused as to whether they were at the right church. Why were there so many seemingly same-sex couples sitting around the building? Many of them would look over at their colleagues and give them that ***"questioning"*** look. Others would just kind of shrug a shoulder or shake their head side to side in response. They didn't have a clue, either. It became obvious they had had no idea that Don D. was Gay. They had worked with him for over 25 years and never really knew him.

The real giveaway was when Al got up to speak. There had been a nice little service about Don D. and what he had done for the church, and about God's love. The choir had sung some of Don D.'s favorite hymns. There was a really nice portrait of Don D. at the altar area, and his urn was under it. I had been sitting behind Al for support. When he got up, I squeezed his shoulder and told him he could do this.

When he got up to the front of the room by Don D.'s portrait, he picked up Don D.'s ashes, stood next to his portrait, and thanked everyone for coming to honor his life partner. (They had been together about six years by this time.) As soon as he called Don D. his life partner, you could almost hear a room full of jaws hit the floor in shock. Suddenly, there was a lot of shifting in seats and heads turning. It was very obvious that none of his co-workers had had a clue, which made me curious if they would have accepted him if he had been openly Gay.

Don D. was in his 50s and this was in the mid 1990s. Like so many of the members of the church, he had grown up in the time you didn't make your lifestyle public in any way. You could very possibly be thrown out of school, lose your job, be disowned by your family, get the crap beaten out of you, or even killed. So that's when it dawned on me what he had meant when he told the doctor, "This was my fate from God because of what I am, and I accepted it." He thought God had punished him for being Gay. That is what mainstream churches had always told Gay people—***especially the children***—so they wouldn't grow up to be Gay. They wanted to instill fear into the children and teach them that God hated them and would smite them with cruelty.

Imagine how many lives of good, decent people of faith have been damaged—***or even ended***—based on such ideas!

I am grateful that Don D. helped build a safe church for Gay people to congregate, but I feel sad that he still believed what he had been taught by ignorant people. I am also glad that things are changing for the better. Sometimes it seems like only a little bit here and there, but changing for the better, nonetheless.

CHAPTER TWENTY-ONE
LITTLE BARB'S, WHIT'S, AND AL'S CELEBRATIONS OF LIFE

We lost Little Barb and Whit in 2023, and we lost Al in 2024. I was able to make it to Little Barb's and Whit's ceremony, but not Al's. I heard it was beautiful. All three of them received beautiful Celebrations of Life at the church. I spoke at Little Barb's, telling some of the funny things that I've included in this book, such as the night I met her. I was also at Whit's, and I asked David if I could say something at some point. He said, "I was hoping you would." I recognized some of the faces, but most of the members that had been there when I was were gone, and the crowd had a lot of newer members. None of them knew much about the construction of the building.

I proceeded telling some stories about Whit—primarily the day I met him at the big metal building, when Little Barb introduced me to him. Remember, she told him I might be able to help the congregation, and his response was, "I'll believe it when I see it!" Then there was the story of his tunneling to the other bathroom. David started laughing. "I remember when I found out what he was doing and I went to see him just in time to see his little butt just disappear below the concrete." Everyone got a good chuckle out of that. Another person spoke about Whit and how he looked forward to Pride at Disney World every year. He just loved all the colors and the energy, and he couldn't see everything fast enough. That sounded about right for him. He loved life!

It's always nice to go to a Celebration of Life when it is truly a celebration of their life. Whit was quite a character. Not like a comedian-funny character, but just his personality being so unique, his love of life, and his commitment to the church and anyone who needed him. He was truly a good soul, and David is as well. They were together for 45 years before Whit died.

I wanted to go to Al's Celebration of Life. I wanted to tell people some of the stories you see in this book and most importantly to make them aware that he had constructed the memorial trail around the property and the stained glass windows over the pulpit area. They would have enjoyed the story about him asking who was coming in to do what project next, and never realizing that he and the rest were the ones coming! He never complained. He loved that church and everyone in it.

After Don D. passed, Al grieved for a long time until he met Tim. He and Tim were together for a very long time. Al was still in very good physical condition, but after a couple of years, Al got very sick. Tim was such a great husband. He took care of Al for at least 12 years that I can think of, until he died in 2024.

I also want to add that Big Barb recently died, in July of 2025. Her family had moved her to the West Coast to be closer to loved ones who would be able to take care of her. She had been in a nursing home for a number of years, but she was never forgotten. David contacted me to tell me of her passing. I was pleased that I was being kept in the loop among those who had been there for the creation of the church and building.

At the beginning of this book, I told you that Little Barb was my right-hand person in coordinating the materials, dealing with the engineer and building department, and so many other things. I was so grateful for both the Barbs working with me.

I also want to thank David for his contributions during the construction of the church. He and Whit had been the main participants in the creation of the church. They both showed up every Saturday for work days and never complained about any project I put them on. The Barbs, David and Whit, and Don D. and Al were there every work day and were hugely helpful in keeping the property mowed and cleaned up.

Now, it is just David and me. We are the last ones who had been so involved with making this church happen. To this day, David still goes to the church for services, thirty-plus years since the completion of the construction. He was a very big helper in the construction, and I wanted to thank him for being such a huge help for me in writing this book, because he had all the knowledge of the creation of the church from day one.

Me and David at Big Barb's Celebration of LIfe, 2026

David was the primary source for many of the stories, experiences, and processes that went on before I started working on the church. It was not always an easy task for us, trying to remember some of the details after thirty-plus years! Both of us are now seniors, so our memories had to be shook up every now and then.

I pray that members continue coming in to keep that church alive and support Catherine as their reverend. Maybe this book will make more people more aware of it and they'll start attending, or at least watch the live YouTube services. You can learn about events and location of the church and property by visiting https://www.youtube.com/@trinity_mcc_gainesville/featured.

In my construction career of over 40 years, I have built around 149 buildings and rehabbed over 2,000 homes—but this project was the most memorable, fulfilling, life-changing, and important to me. I know it was truly a gift from God to allow me to work with those wonderful people on the building. It was a gift to be part of such a purposeful community project and to be a part of the changes of that time. ***Amen.***

EPILOGUE

Since the construction of the church has been completed, it has truly made an impact on the community at large. The church hosts quilting groups that have made over 600 quilts to distribute to the homeless. They have also made and distributed blessing bags with food, water, and personal grooming items for unsheltered homeless to hand them out of car windows quickly when in traffic – as well as specialty bags for homeless women, to supply pads, tampons and other hygiene items.

The church has also established an Unconditional Love Fund as a portion of their larger General Endowment Fund. The Unconditional Love Fund provides emergency funds to students who are cut off from their families after they come out to them as LGBTQ.

With the guidance of Reverend Dearlove, so many people who attend TMCC do charitable things such as collecting aluminum cans for the Deacons' Fund and creating a food bank for the parishioners needing temporary help. Parishioners bring canned or boxed foods for those who need the help. They also donate soda can tops to the Ronald McDonald House of Gainesville, a non-profit providing temporary housing and support for families with critically ill children being treated at area medical facilities. TMCC has marched and sung in Pride Festivals, parades, and picnics—and even ran Bingo at the Pride Center!

AFTERWORD

~

Anybody can make contributions to this church, to any particular fund you prefer.
https://www.mccgainesville.org/donate

~

ABOUT THE AUTHOR

Judy is a new author, who at a young age discovered her construction and engineering skills and gifted them to a relatively new congregation. Her memoir recalls the progress toward building a permanent home for an often-rejected LGBTQ community and her own evolving spirituality. The arriving of Judy's leadership and vision to transfer a partially complete quonset hut into a sacred worship space for Trinity Metropolitan Community Church was truly Providential. As a member of the all-volunteer work crew looking back over decades since digging the building foundation, I wonder at how much of our determination was Divinely driven and how much was a reaction to the evolving movement to proclaim our identity as a worthy LGBTQ community. Either way, Judy Raymond's memoir documents the historical record within the context of society's view of LGBTQ people together with her personal journey of discovery, which included her calling to build a church along with gaining insight into her spirituality.

-- *David D. Williams, PhD*

www.ingramcontent.com/pod-product-compliance
Lightning Source LLC
LaVergne TN
LVHW011031110826
845149LV00015B/3373

* 9 7 9 8 9 9 6 0 1 3 7 1 5 *